100 Years of Architecture
at Notre Dame

100 Years of Architecture at Notre Dame

...

A HISTORY OF THE SCHOOL OF ARCHITECTURE
1898–1998

BOND HALL

EDITED BY JANE A. DEVINE

The School of Architecture gratefully acknowledges the support of Charles J. Toeniskoetter and Dan L. Breeding, Toeniskoetter & Breeding Inc., who funded the printing of this book.

Cover artwork by David J. Cutler, Class of 1999

Printed in the United States of America

Printing by Mossberg & Co. Inc., South Bend, Indiana

This book is printed on acid-free paper.

ISBN 0-9670548-0-X

Table of Contents

About the Contributors   vi

A Message from the President — *Rev. Edward A. Malloy, C.S.C.*   vii

Foreword: A Century of Constancy and Change — *Carroll William Westfall*   viii

Preface and Acknowledgements — *Jane A. Devine*   x

Between Two Centuries: A History of the School, 1898–1998 — *John W. Stamper*   1

Housing the Architects: From the Dome to Bond Hall — *Norman A. Crowe*   25

The Golden Chain: The Kervick-Montana Years — *Dennis P. Doordan*   37

Up 100 Steps for Architecture: A Student Memoir from 1928 — *C. Arnold Thoma*   48

A Glance Back — *Robert L. Amico*   51

Reconnecting With Classicism — *Thomas Gordon Smith*   61

By the Book: A History of the Architecture Library — *Jane A. Devine*   65

A Chronology of Important Events   74

Faculty Roster   77

Graduates Roster   80

Table of Illustrations   104

Index   106

About the Contributors

ROBERT L. AMICO was chairman of the School of Architecture from 1978 to 1989. He now teaches fifth-year design studio and is active in professional practice.

NORMAN A. CROWE teaches environmental studies and design studio in the School of Architecture, where he joined the faculty in 1974. He is the author of *Nature and the Idea of a Man-made World: An Investigation into the Evolutionary Roots of Form and Order in the Built Environment* (1995) and *Visual Notes for Architects and Designers* (1984).

JANE A. DEVINE became architecture and art librarian at Notre Dame in 1997. She has contributed to several films and publications as a writer, bibliographer, translator and researcher.

DENNIS P. DOORDAN has taught architectural history at Notre Dame since 1990. He is coeditor of the journal *Design Issues*. His other writings include *Design History: An Anthology* (1995) and *Building Modern Italy: Italian Architecture, 1914–1936* (1988).

THOMAS GORDON SMITH was chairman of the School of Architecture from 1989 to 1998. He is a practicing architect and the author of *Classical Architecture: Rule and Invention* (1988).

JOHN W. STAMPER joined the faculty in 1984. He has been director of the Rome Studies Center since 1990 and teaches architectural history there. *Chicago's North Michigan Avenue: Planning and Development, 1900–1930* (1991) is among his publications.

C. ARNOLD THOMA received his bachelor of architecture degree from Notre Dame in 1928. He is retired from practice and lives in Dayton, Ohio.

CARROLL WILLIAM WESTFALL became the Frank Montana professor and chairman of the School of Architecture in 1998. His books include *Architectural Principles in the Age of Historicism* (1991) and *In This Most Perfect Paradise; Alberti, Nicholas V, and the Invention of Conscious Urban Planning in Rome, 1447–55* (1974).

OFFICE OF THE PRESIDENT
UNIVERSITY OF NOTRE DAME

February 1999

Dear Friends,

   I join you with great enthusiasm as we commemorate the 100th anniversary of the University of Notre Dame School of Architecture. We celebrate this occasion as we look back in time and reflect on the strides we have made in providing a quality education to students nationally and around the world in the field of architecture. This special commemorative book guides us through this history as we revive the past, marvel at the present and look forward to the future. Many thanks to those who have contributed to the collective memory of the rich and progressive history of the School of Architecture.

   The University of Notre Dame was the first Catholic university in the United States to offer an architecture degree. We led the way in the development of an architectural curriculum designed to meet the academic and professional needs of aspiring architects. For the past 100 years, the School of Architecture has prepared students to enter into a highly competitive world marketplace. We are the only school to require a year in Rome as an integral part of the students' education in architecture and urbanism. There are over 2,000 graduates of the program who are working not only in the United States, but also in Japan, Europe and Latin America. The impact of our program is widespread.

   One Hundred Years of Architecture at Notre Dame: A History of the School of Architecture 1898–1998 is the story of the collaborative efforts of faculty, administrators, staff, students and alumni who have contributed to the life of the School of Architecture throughout the years. The high personal standard and commitment to the field of architecture by these individuals have greatly contributed to a program of which we can all be proud. My congratulations and best wishes to the School of Architecture as we look forward to another 100 years.

Cordially,

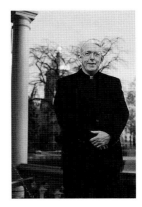

(Rev.) Edward A. Malloy, C.S.C.
President

Foreword

A Century of Constancy and Change

■ ■ ■

CARROLL WILLIAM WESTFALL

Frank Montana Professor and Chairman
School of Architecture

Change has been one major animating force in the Western tradition, and discovering the constancy within change has been another. We accept change as a constant within the world, but what we make of it forces us to make a choice between constancy and change. We can revel in the change and neglect that which endures within the change, or we can focus on the enduring while enjoying the diversity and variety enlivening the enduring.

Reveling in change atomizes experience and leads to relativism. Embracing the enduring establishes links to other fields of human endeavor. The former, which has champions ranging from Heraclitus to the modernists and their heirs, reaches no further than the secular world. The latter, which constitutes the central theme of the Judeo-Hellenic-Christian tradition, embraces the widest range of secular life, and it necessarily encompasses the sacred life as well.

Notre Dame would be a poor host to Heraclitus and the modernists. As a Catholic university, its educational program is founded on the acceptance that there is truth, that truth endures across times and within different secular and sacred traditions, and that one of our most worthy purposes is to learn that truth for oneself and act on that knowledge. Furthermore, it recognizes that that truth comes from God and is accessible to us through the gifts God gave us, those of reason, memory, and an innate, unique talent that enables us to seek and manifest the truth for the assistance of others.

One of those talents is the talent required to practice architecture. Theorists from Vitruvius onward agree that architecture is best served if people lacking that talent avoid architecture. The first Christian theorist went further: Leon Battista Alberti, the first architect involved in designing the present complex of church and palace at the Vatican, explained that those who have the talent to be architects and fail to use it, or who use it without cultivating it in order to use it well, are as distant from God's favor as those who lack the talent but act as if they have it.

Carroll William Westfall

The highest and best use of the talent required for architecture is that of revealing truth. Truth endures, and so does architecture. Those who accept truth as their guide recognize that God spoke no one language, that the liturgy is limited to no one form, and that no single manner of organizing society is the single true and right form. So too in architecture: Those who practice architecture as a form of revealing truth recognize that the truth in architecture exists not in any particular form or style and certainly not in any particular building. Architecture, like other forms truth can take — justice, beauty, goodness — endures in the skillful and well-wrought products of those who are devoted to allowing the matrix of truth to guide their actions.

Reason, another gift of God, makes possible a rational and therefore human linkage between architecture and other forms of endeavor. That linkage is not possible if reason is held hostage by the passions, by instinct, by impulses, by solipsistic referents, or by other forms of the irrational or nonreason sanctioned by a continuous stream of proponents running from Heraclitus to the postmodernists. Without reason as the foundation for the study of architecture, there is no place for architecture within a university worthy of the name.

And so too with memory. Memory, or tradition, allows the efforts of earlier colleagues to guide us in the present. When we know tradition, we know where to start and how to proceed. When we know tradition, we know the standards of excellence we must aspire to reach. When we know tradition, we know where architecture is to be found within the welter of buildings we have inherited from the past.

But reason and tradition can be as dangerous to the architect as gifts left uncultivated if they are not governed by purely human qualities. To avoid the false safety of certainty available within merely rational argument and the legacy of well-learned tradition, reason and memory must be tempered with the compassion of the heart and the moral sense God gave us.

Therefore, at Notre Dame, recognizing that architecture has a particular role to play within an explicitly Catholic university has never meant that a building is like a dogmatic pronouncement or other *obiter dictum.* There is no "Catholic style" of architecture, just as there is no particular style unique to or appropriate for tyranny, democracy, capitalism, "the West" and so on. An architecture based on truth manifests the best skill possible, imitates the nature of a world founded on reason, and embodies the traditions appropriate to the purpose, people and place it is serving. And it does more: It makes manifest the presence of God's grace in the world.

Architecture at Notre Dame has not been rooted in dogma, but neither has it been static. The program has constantly changed, but reason and tradition have ballasted it through a century more notable for reveling in change than for embracing the enduring. The result is impressive: For a century Notre Dame has honed the skills of those equipped to be architects, and its graduates have gone forth to produce buildings that assist people in living nobly and well within a society that recognizes that in their daily lives, the secular and the sacred are constantly intersecting. May it do so for at least another century.

Preface and Acknowledgements

I first became interested in the history of the School of Architecture as a newcomer to Notre Dame in the fall of 1997. As I met the alumni who returned to campus and visited the Architecture Library, many had questions about classmates or former faculty and fascinating stories to tell about their experiences as students.

It soon became clear that a full history of the architecture program had never been written. Some preliminary research in the University Archives revealed that almost no complete institutional records remained, aside from the files of certain faculty members or documents from brief periods in the school's life. Instead the history of the program was interwoven with that of the University, and valuable information could be gleaned from reports, course bulletins, yearbooks, student newspapers and the files of important individuals. The physical memory of the program could be found in a scattering of historical photographs and in the buildings where it had been housed, all of which fortunately still exist. Realizing that 1998–99 marked the centenary of the degree in architecture, it seemed the ideal occasion to create a lasting record that will serve those interested in the past and also future researchers who want as complete a picture as possible of the Notre Dame School of Architecture's unique history.

Once I was convinced that a history could be written, the next stage was to find the contributors to make the project a success. John Stamper, director of the Rome Studies Center, had already done work in this area and readily agreed to write the leading essay. Likewise, Norman Crowe had researched the history of Bond Hall and was willing to complete his study with a look at the various buildings the school had occupied. Dennis Doordan became intrigued by the role of the two longest-serving chairmen, Francis Kervick and Frank Montana, in shaping the program's direction and offered to develop this theme in his essay. I felt that a history of the Architecture Library would also be a valuable chapter in the overall story. Through alumnus

Bob Canizaro, whose father, James, was in the class of 1928, a wonderful memoir from the same year came to light: C. Arnold Thoma's lively account of student escapades and late nights in the studio will appeal to all architecture students who have shared that universal experience. Lastly, Thomas Gordon Smith and Bob Amico agreed to offer their thoughts on directions in the school under their respective chairmanships. All of these contributors explore different aspects and periods, providing a range of viewpoints that deepens our understanding of the school's history.

To guide the planning of the book, we then formed an editorial committee consisting of professors Norman Crowe, Dennis Doordan, Richard Economakis and, later, William Westfall. With the contributors and advisory committee in place, all that remained was to find a sponsor for the book and to start the work of researching and compiling the various sections. Incoming chairman Westfall was immediately encouraging and presented the project to the School of Architecture Advisory Council. Charles J. Toeniskoetter and Dan L. Breeding of Toeniskoetter & Breeding Inc. answered our appeal with a very generous donation that funded printing of the book. Without their financial support, we could not have prepared to go to press in just five short months.

A few words about editorial policy: I have tried to respect historical accuracy in the names of people, buildings and events. What is now the School of Architecture has been previously known as the Course in Architecture, the College of Architecture, and the Department of Architecture. As much as possible, we have used the correct designation for the appropriate time period, but in some cases the terms "school" or "program" are used in a general sense. When referring to buildings on campus, we have tried to use the official names of the period with the contemporary name in parentheses where names have changed. Certain faculty members' names exist in variant spellings, so I have adopted the most commonly used form as the official name. All the dates given for events have been carefully checked in archival sources, although published records sometimes contradict them. With these caveats in mind, I hope the book is as accurate as it possibly can be, particularly given the paucity of sources that we had to overcome.

This volume aims to be both a thoughtful written account and a visual record of the School of Architecture. Images are as important as words, often even more so in the study of architecture. With that in mind, the book collects not only thematic essays but also a wide variety of images from the University Archives, past Notre Dame publications and the private collections of people connected to the school. These glimpses of students, faculty and the process of becoming architects, shown in classroom scenes and student drawings, provide a visual history of the school's progress that complements and enriches the essays. I hope alumni and professors will find a reflection of themselves in these pages and that readers outside Notre Dame will gain an appreciation of our place in the history of architectural education.

Many people have had a hand in this book's creation, and they all deserve heartfelt thanks for their contributions:

— archivists Charles Lamb and Peter Lysy, University of Notre Dame Archives, for their work in finding photographs, documents and obscure records of the school's past and for their infinite patience in answering arcane questions as we combed the files for missing details

— Marten Schalm, University of Notre Dame Publications and Graphic Services, for his outstanding graphic design work and creative advice on every stage of the book's layout

— Kathryn Schuth, class of 1999, for her diligence and meticulous research work sifting through many sources to find images, names and information to support the main contributors' work and the compilation of the faculty roster

— David Cutler, class of 1999, for the beautiful watercolors that adorn the cover

— alumnus C. Arnold Thoma for his evocative memoir of student life in 1928

— Ida Bonicelli, her daughter Mary Yolanda Trigiani and Geri Decker for sharing their recollections and photographs of the Architecture Library

— Prof. Tom Schlereth for his advice in the early days of the project and his expertise in reviewing the history of the School of Architecture's three homes

— Ellen Skerrett, an independent scholar in Chicago, who found us the only known photograph of Henry John Schlacks when he was director of the architecture degree program

— the Archdiocese of Chicago for graciously allowing us to reprint the Schlacks photograph

— alumnus Bob Canizaro for his help in retracing aspects of the 1960s in the school and for lending photographs from his personal collection

— Christian Dupont and Rita Erskine, University Libraries Department of Special Collections, for their assistance in finding library reports and early course bulletins

— Charlotte Ames, University Libraries Catholic Americana bibliographer, for her help in researching Francis Kervick's writings

— Father Richard Bullene, C.S.C., for contributing pictures of his student year in Rome

— Professor emeritus Frank Montana, whose drawings from his time as Paris Prize winner and Rome director are featured in two of the essays

— David Williams for his painstaking work creating a database of over 2,100 graduates from the official commencement programs and for supervising data entry by Architecture Library student assistants Timothy Borgen, Mekashia Chenault, Sarah Hammes, Renita Riley and Richard Salinas

Most of all, my thanks to Joanne Bessler, assistant director for User Services, University Libraries, for encouraging my work on this project from the beginning, and to my staff, Deborah Webb, Margaret Turza and David Williams, for their support and enthusiasm during the book's preparation.

— *Jane A. Devine, Editor*

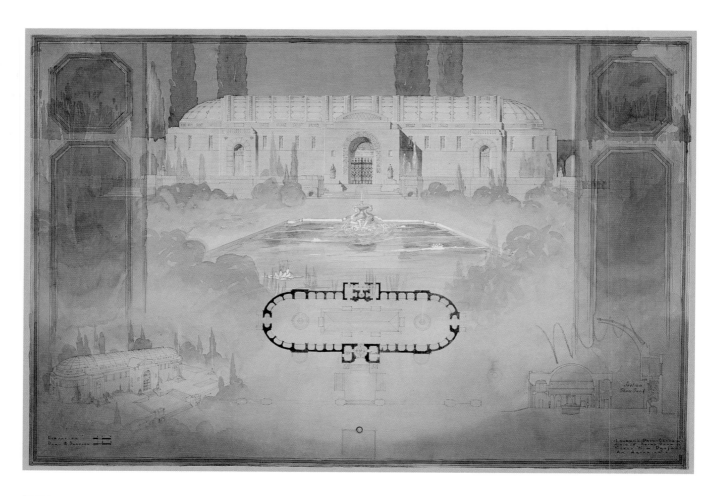

Figure 1.

Laurens Paul Cotter. An Aquarium. Elevation, plan and section. Mention, Beaux-Arts Institute of Design
Department of Architecture, Class "B" IV Projet, 1929.

Between Two Centuries:

A History of the School, 1898–1998

■ ■ ■

JOHN W. STAMPER

Architects who without culture aim at manual skill cannot gain a prestige corresponding to their labors, while those who trust to theory and literature obviously follow a shadow and not reality. But those who have mastered both, like men equipped in full armour, soon acquire influence and attain their purpose.

— Vitruvius, THE TEN BOOKS OF ARCHITECTURE

To study architecture requires a commitment. To study architecture at Notre Dame requires a special commitment — not only to the goals of a professional education but also to the values and ideals offered by a liberal arts curriculum that includes both philosophy and theology as an integral part of intellectual and theoretical training. But more than that, it demands a commitment of its students to follow the goals of a classical education. Distinguishing itself from other American and European university programs, Notre Dame emphasizes a study of traditional architecture — its building methods, its way of forming urban space, its definition of aesthetic value — as an alternative to the dominant education model.

Recognizing the destruction of urban architecture in the United States that has been brought about by the planning, building and development practices of the past 50 years, the Notre Dame School of Architecture seeks to provide a different method, one with new goals, the intent being to improve the city, not merely gesture to its ironies and contradictions or relativize its history. Such an approach is closely linked to the context of practice in Renaissance Europe, whose roots can be traced to ancient Greece and Rome, Ictinus and Callicrates, and of course, Vitruvius. But it is also linked to the more recent history of both the École des Beaux-Arts and the City Beautiful Movement, which set the

immediate context for the founding of the school at the end of the 19th century. The
Beaux-Arts method as it was introduced into the United States by Richard Morris Hunt
and William Ware, the Court of Honor of the World's Columbian Exposition of 1893,
and the City Beautiful Movement of Daniel Burnham, Charles McKim and Frederick
Law Olmsted Jr., were the most important influences on the school in the first years
of its existence, and it is to these precedents that the school looks today.

For the scores of young men and women who traverse the United States and other
countries each year to come to South Bend, settle into the neo-Gothic dormitories
of the Notre Dame campus, and begin their undergraduate education among the
University's community of teachers, scholars, priests and administrators, it requires
a special vision, a goal that is somehow different from that of students in most other
disciplines. They are not motivated by money, not even necessarily by prestige, but
by a passion for buildings, and above all, a commitment to the manmade world, its
development, its betterment, and even its beauty. They envision themselves as
stewards of the city, its civic buildings, its schools and churches, its residential neigh-
borhoods, its public places. They put these things above their own personal comfort,
much like the young priests of the Congregation of Holy Cross who commit their lives
to the service of the community and its spiritual development. Dedication to the cause
of their profession, whether architects or priests, has always been their deepest
motivation.

The Notre Dame campus is a special place for its architecture students. It is their
first "city" in that most of them grew up in small towns or middle-class suburbs and
have never known the qualities of a collegiate setting. They have never before experienced a planned pedestrian zone with vast open spaces framed by historic buildings
and centered around a great domed building and a Gothic basilica. They have never
before lived in a city populated with other citizens their own age, which gives them the
opportunity to interact in a Socratic way with a community of educators, and which
provides for them a world-class library aimed at opening their minds to the complexi-
ties of the world and its history. Above all, it is their first architectural challenge, the
place where they receive their first instruction in drawing, in architectural history, in
the fundamentals of design. It is the site of their architectural training, the place where
they learn to see the built world through different eyes; and as such, it becomes the
visual context of their design work for the rest of their careers, the reference they will
always come back to when visualizing new spaces and structures.

N otre Dame was the first Catholic university in the United States to
establish a program and award a degree in architecture. Courses
in drawing and design were offered as early as 1869, though the
degree-granting program was not formally initiated until 1898.
Becoming the College of Architecture in 1906, it offered bachelor
and master of science degrees in architecture and in architectural engineering. Later,
it became a department in the College of Engineering, and its undergraduate program,
like most others in the country, was expanded to five years.

It further distinguished itself in 1969 by initiating a junior-year-abroad program,
becoming the only American university to offer a yearlong program of study for
architecture in Rome, Italy. Throughout its history the School has been closely linked
to the multiplicity of contemporary architectural traditions — neoclassicism, Gothic
Revival, Modernism, Postmodernism, New Classicism — that have characterized the
20th century. But more than that, its students have been influenced by the unique

qualities of the University's administration, board of trustees, religious staff and faculty, all of whom have consistently exhibited a blend of cultural and moral values informed on the one hand by the Catholic Church and on the other by a keen interest in European traditions and thought. It is these men and women who have guided the development of both the students' manual skills and their theoretical training just as Vitruvius had advised more than 2,000 years ago.

Architectural education in the mid-19th century, both in the United States and in Europe, was very different from today's broad-based five- and six-year professional programs. The lack of educational opportunities reflected the general disorder evident in the building profession itself. There were no clear-cut distinctions between architects, builders and engineers. Anyone with the ability and the backing of a client could operate at any level of the building industry, from design to construction, whatever their qualifications and training. The profession then ran the gamut from architects working as developers, to lawyers with a staff of draftsmen working as architects, to surveyors working as carpenters. The industry as a whole was in chaos, with no regulating standards to organize production, competitions and contractual arrangements between owners and architects.[1] Architect Henry Van Brunt wrote:

> The study of architecture at that time was pursued under the
> most discouraging conditions. The art was ill understood and indeed
> hardly respected by the public. There were no schools in which it
> was recognized as a desirable subject for study. There were but few
> books available and our traditions were eminently provincial.[2]

For those few American architects who had both the will and the financial means to study abroad, the French École des Beaux-Arts, founded in 1671 to groom architects for careers in the civil service and to design monumental public buildings, offered the most comprehensive course of study, not just in architectural design but also in mathematics, construction, perspective, and fortification design.[3] The teaching of design took place in independent studios, or ateliers, whose masters were well-known Parisian architects. Students attending such ateliers received criticism for their projects — which were usually in the form of competitions — not only from the studio heads, but from other more advanced students as well. Their progress was measured by the quality of their work rather than by periods of time or specific classes, and endowed prizes served to motivate their work in what was an intensely competitive system.[4] The first American to study at the École des Beaux-Arts, and the first to introduce its principles of architecture and architectural education into the United States, was Richard Morris Hunt.

Noted for his design of the Morgan Library and the first building of the Metropolitan Museum of Art in New York, Hunt's greatest legacy was his introduction into the United States during the early 1860s of the French method of apprenticing in an atelier, of working and studying with a master trained in the classical orders and the Beaux-Arts system of design. For those who did not have the advantage of a proper French education, the opportunity to apprentice in Hunt's office was the next best thing.[5] He provided the most enlightened mentorship at the time, using both his talent and extensive library to inspire his young apprentices in the ideals and details of classical architecture.[6] Such a means of acquiring design proficiency and technical knowledge for those entering the architectural profession at times produced genius, while at others resulted in intermittent and uncoordinated training. Outside the small circle of Hunt's office, relatively few architects were able to bring to their work the technical skills and broader cultural advantages that could be provided either by college training or by study abroad.[7]

As architects began to organize their profession and to concern themselves with standards within the increasingly complex challenges posed by the building trades, the need for formal architectural training in the United States became evident. The first university to respond to the need was the Massachusetts Institute of Technology, which established in 1867 the country's first educational program in architecture. Its first director was William Robert Ware, who had been one of Hunt's students, and had then developed a successful practice in Boston with Henry Van Brunt, also a Hunt protégé. Their office, which they had modeled after Hunt's, had likewise become an important training ground for a generation of younger architects.[8] Ware's book, *The American Vignola,* which codified the orders for the American classical Renaissance of the 19th and early 20th centuries, became one of the leading textbooks for architectural training.[9]

When Ware initiated the program at MIT, he adapted to American needs the methods of both Hunt and the École, a program that was further strengthened by the hiring in 1872 of the French-trained Eugène Létang to direct the design studios. Students learned by executing set projects in competition and by progressing through a series of ever more difficult design problems, involving an increasingly wider range of conditions and areas of design. As in the École method, there was an emphasis on building plans in the belief that a good plan inevitably resulted in both a handsome and functional building. Above all, architectural drawing was the focus of all the students' work: tracing, copying, graphic construction, penwork, brushwork, outdoor sketching, and the study of the orders.[10] The significant difference between the French educational model and the way it was adopted by Ware and Létang was to respond to the far less monumental conditions of practice in the United States and to provide a broader education for the students, developing especially their understanding of architectural history.[11]

Shortly after Ware founded the MIT program, the concept of organized training in architecture caught on at other universities. A second school was established at the University of Illinois at Urbana-Champaign in January 1870, with courses of instruction being directed by the first European teacher in an American school, Harold M. Hansen, a Swedish architect trained at the Bau Akademie in Berlin.[12] In 1871, Cornell University was the third institution to establish an architecture school, directed by Charles Babcock, a liberal arts graduate of Union College and a partner of the New York architect Richard M. Upjohn.[13] Each of these three schools produced their first graduates in 1873: Henry A. Phillips at MIT, Nathan Clifford Ricker at Illinois, and John R. Schoonover at Cornell.

Six other programs were founded in the next two decades, at Syracuse, Pennsylvania, Michigan, Columbia, George Washington and the Armour Institute of Technology. In 1895, Harvard established its architecture curriculum as a part of the Lawrence Scientific Institute.[14] Its director, Herbert Langford Warren, trained by Ware and Létang at MIT, and author of the book *The Foundations of Classic Architecture,* inspired, according to historian and architect Fiske Kimball, "a generation of architects who have striven to design buildings that represent knowledge, order, and classic beauty."[15]

The good intentions of all of the university programs were handicapped, however, by a number of factors: inadequate secondary schools, a suspicion by many practitioners of a formal education and by a general lack of financial resources. Even though there were nearly a dozen schools established by the late 1890s, there were only 360 students enrolled in architecture across the country. Columbia had the largest group

with 78, but the average enrollment in the rest of the schools was about 40. During their first three decades, the nation's architecture schools had trained only a fraction of the 10,581 architects reported in the 1900 census.[16]

The primary influence on the schools at the end of the century was the attention given to architecture and urban design during the World's Columbian Exposition in Chicago in 1893, an event that marked the first time in the history of the United States that architects had an opportunity to plan such a large group of buildings as an ensemble, the first time to place such buildings in an environment of gardens, fountains and sculpture at such a large scale. The impression the fair made on visitors, including professionals and student architects, was extraordinary and nearly universally positive. For the period of the 1890s, Daniel Burnham and his east coast collaborators unquestionably attained a great achievement: They succeeded in expressing in architectural terms a vision for the future shared by a majority of Americans.

Part of the intention of the fair's designers was to provide an instructive example to untutored architects as a way of promoting a revival of the classical style, which had been displaced in the 1870s and '80s by alternatives like the Second Empire and Romanesque Revival. They wanted to show the need for discipline and knowledge in architecture in what Van Brunt called a "scenic display, composed — to use the theatrical term — of 'practicable' models, executed on a colossal stage. . . ."[17] These architects believed strongly in the neoclassical style and, as Burnham stated, they wanted to see its proliferation throughout the country because they thought it was the most appropriate style of the time for the young and growing United States.

Figure 2.
Manufactures and Liberal Arts Building, 1893 World's Columbian Exposition, Chicago, where Notre Dame was part of the Catholic Educational Exhibit.

The influence of the fair was indeed significant on both architecture and urban design in the United States, not to mention on educational programs charged with training the next generation of architects. It did more than any other single factor in the 19th century to encourage aesthetic efforts in municipal life throughout the country, giving tangible shape to the City Beautiful Movement.[18] Burnham's biographer Charles Moore wrote, "the impulse to plan American cities for unity, amenity, and beauty was born of the Exposition."[19] Other expositions reinforced the trend, and there was a mushrooming number of campaigns for comprehensive city planning projects calling for the regularity and monumentality of building design and the fusion of naturalistic park systems with formal neoclassical-style civic centers.[20] Among them were a competition for Copley Square in Boston, a public building group in Cleveland, the McMillan Plan for Washington, D.C., and Philadelphia's Benjamin Franklin Parkway. Most important to Chicago, of course, was Burnham's plan of 1909, in which he proposed rebuilding on a massive scale with a new baroque street pattern, a lakeshore park, and a giant domed civic building based upon Hunt's Administration Building for the fair.

It was within this context that Notre Dame initiated its formal program in architecture in 1898. It was a year in which some of the country's most significant classical buildings were completed: Low Memorial Library at Columbia University by McKim, Mead and White; the Library of Congress by Smithmeyer and Pelz; and nearer at hand, the Public Library in Chicago and the St. Joseph County Courthouse in South Bend, both by Shepley, Rutan and Coolidge. All were projects that, in the words of architectural historian David Hamlin, "lifted our National official architecture from pretentious inferiority to a high level of artistic merit."[21]

Located only 90 miles east of Chicago, Notre Dame was directly influenced by the Columbian Exposition in both its architecture and educational method. The University had participated in the fair with an exhibit of 120 photographs of the campus and samples of student work. Father John Zahm, a scientist and University vice president, had initially tried to buy the Machinery Hall of the Exposition, planning to have it dismantled and then reassembled on the Notre Dame campus to be used by the engineering departments. Failing in this, he persuaded the administration to build Crowley Hall in 1893 to house what was then called the Institute of Technology. In 1897 the first bachelor's degree in electrical engineering was granted and in 1899 the first in mechanical engineering.

It was in this climate of academic growth that Notre Dame's architecture course was established as a degree program in 1898–99. Its first quarters were in the well-lit, double-height space next to the art department on the fifth floor of the Administration Building, a huge multipurpose structure built in the Victorian Gothic style by Chicago architect Willoughby J. Edbrooke in 1879. Containing offices, living quarters, classrooms, dining rooms, the library, and art studios, it was the centerpiece of Notre Dame's 1,400-acre campus.[22]

At the time of the founding of Notre Dame's architecture program, the city of South Bend had a population of about 50,000. The Notre Dame campus was, and remains, a relatively isolated location for the study of architecture in comparison to the dense urban settings of MIT or Columbia. A trolley line, running from South Bend to Niles, Michigan, passed through the grounds, although visits to either city were not favored by the University administration because of the desire to "guard against loss of time and possible exposure to 'temptations.'"[23] While such a policy had clear advantages for the students' safety and moral development, it allowed the architecture students little

Figure 3.
Architecture drafting studio on the Administration Building's fifth floor, 1914.

opportunity for urban involvement. The pastoral quality of the landscaped campus, something more akin to a 19th-century suburban setting or the University of Virginia Quad, has always been the context within which the architecture students have worked.

Virtually all of the students resided on campus, as they still do today, and they traditionally developed a great camaraderie, an enduring quality of the Notre Dame experience. The total student population at the University in the 1890s numbered about 700 a year, all males, and all but 20 percent of them Catholic.[24] While the geographical distribution of the students was relatively limited in the early years, it has since become one of the most widely diverse of any private university in the country.

The first formal courses in architecture were taught by Henry John Schlacks, a successful Chicago church architect, who came to South Bend once a week to supervise the students' work, assisted by Francis Xavier Ackerman, head of the Department of Mechanical Drawing.[25] Schlacks served as the director of the architecture department from 1903 to 1905, a period notable for two major events in the history of classical architecture in the United States: the completion of the much-lauded Rhode Island State Capitol by McKim, Mead and White, and the staging of the Louisiana Purchase Exposition in St. Louis. Schlacks introduced into the curriculum a rigorous Beaux-Arts system like that of MIT (where he had studied), Harvard and the other Eastern schools and commensurate with the influence of the Columbian Exposition and the City Beautiful Movement.[26] As Fikret Yegül states in his book *Gentlemen of Instinct and Breeding: Architecture at the American Academy in Rome,* it was thought by most educators that by studying specifically the classical orders, the needs of the profession for higher social standing and higher artistic and technical standards would be met. Teaching design through a study of classical precedents was thought the best way to solve modern problems.[27]

Figure 4.
Henry John Schlacks

Figure 5.
Francis Xavier Ackerman

7

Figure 6.

The art department studio on the Administration Building's fifth floor, with its collection of plaster casts, 1905.

Early architectural design courses in the department consisted of drawing and rendering in pen and ink and watercolors. They focused especially on the elements employed in classical, Renaissance and Gothic design, though the former was stressed the most. In conjunction with studies of the orders, the students were taught the principles of planning and composition, and design of monumental structures.[28] As Yegül writes, the view at the turn of the century was that classical and Renaissance styles of architecture represented the most refined taste and that they were the most suitable for the future needs of America.[29]

While classicism was clearly the dominant focus in the design studio, reflecting the near hegemony it had within the profession, architectural history courses at Notre Dame were another matter. They included lectures on the Egyptian, Greek, Roman, Byzantine, Gothic and Renaissance periods, reflecting a theoretical approach that in itself was at odds with the method of the École studio system. Harvard's Herbert Langford Warren wrote in 1899 that while the teaching at the École was superior to any other, it was nevertheless

> . . . narrow, so that those brought up exclusively under its influence
> were generally strangely ignorant of all forms of architecture except
> those which were traditional within the school. They had made no
> adequate study of the historic styles and so had no understanding or
> appreciation of the way in which the immutable principles of design
> expressed themselves in other forms and under other conditions.
> Their experience was so narrow that the laws of design could not be
> thoroughly appreciated as the result of principle, and these laws thus
> became, in their hands, little more than a set of academic formulae.[30]

One of the most important architectural history textbooks in the United States was J.-N.-L. Durand's *Recueil et parallèle des édifices de tout genre, anciens et modernes* (1799). Remarkable for its eclecticism, it included examples of Egyptian, Greek, Roman, Chinese, Gothic, Renaissance, Middle Eastern and Indian styles, all juxtaposed in a comparative way as examples of different building types from different countries and periods.[31] Such a comparative study was in part influenced by the first universal history of architecture, the *Entwurff Einer Historischen Architectur,* published by the Austrian baroque architect J.B. Fischer von Erlach in 1721. His comparative history was seen as a sort of scientific study, an objective analysis of the styles of architecture rather than a polemic in favor of a particular mode or process. History was seen as a progressive linear accumulation of experience and data from which the present-day architect could derive principles of architectural design. The *Recueil* was likewise a summary of the experience of the past, which could enable an architect to derive the most correct style.[32] Such an approach has informed the teaching of architectural history at Notre Dame for many decades and has contributed in an important way to its longstanding emphasis on a liberal arts education.

Classes in design and history were complemented by intensive drawing courses taught by Ackerman along with Jobson Emilien Paradis, who had been a pupil in Paris of the neoclassical artist Jean-Léon Gérôme. The system of teaching was intended to instruct students in the principles of classical art while at the same time developing their individuality. The work was done from a combination of casts, objects and nature, including the University buildings, the campus lakes and the St. Joseph River. The art department owned an extensive collection of casts, molded directly from the originals at the École des Beaux-Arts. Many assignments were made specifically for the architects, including drawing from architectural elements such as pedestals, bases, shafts and cornices. Lectures on perspective, art history and the five orders were also given.[33]

The first graduate of the architecture department was Eugenio P. Rayneri y Piedra (1883–1960), who enrolled in December 1899 and received a bachelor of science degree in architectural engineering in 1904. A native of Havana, Cuba, he went on to win first prize in an international competition for the design of the Cuban Presidential Palace in 1910. His most notable work was as technical and artistic director for the construction of the Capitolio in Havana (1929), a spectacular neoclassical building that housed the National Assembly and is today the National Science Library. Rayneri was also the founder and first president of the Cuban Society of Architects (Collegio de Arquitectos) and was decorated by both the Republic of Cuba and the Crown of Italy.[34]

Figure 7.
Eugenio P. Rayneri y Piedra

Figure 8.
Eugenio P. Rayneri y Piedra. First-floor plan of an unnamed building, seemingly an art museum, June 1904.

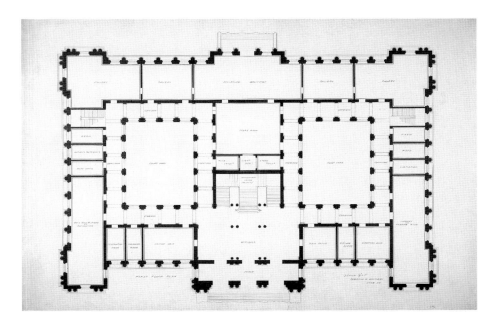

Figure 9.
**Edward Rolland
Adelsperger**

In 1905, South Bend architect Edward Rolland Adelsperger replaced Schlacks as director.[35] Soon afterward, a new College of Architecture was established and an official distinction was made in the curriculum between architectural design and architectural engineering. A one-year graduate program in design, criticism and research was added, leading to the degree master of arts in architecture. For those students following a course in engineering, a curriculum more heavily weighted in mathematics was established, leading to a bachelor of science and a master of science in architectural engineering.[36] The formulation of these specialized degrees was predicated on the idea that architectural design and the science of civil engineering had long outgrown the practical limits of a single individual's ability and that architectural engineering was becoming a significant specialty within the profession. Adelsperger wrote in the 1905 University *Bulletin* that architecture was fundamentally a fine art, but it is a fine art that can be expressed on so large a scale that a deep and comprehensive knowledge of engineering science is necessary to make its expression stable. He went on to state:

> The Master architect is a heaven-gifted man, who having conceived his projects in ultimate beauty of form, color, texture, and ornament, can build them structurally and economically perfect. It is seldom that any mind combines all of these attributes. It is more seldom that today's practice requires them in any one man. Today, one man designs; another frames.[37]

To help support the expanding program, Adelsperger did much to build up its equipment and library collections. There was now a large collection of signed drawings available for study, some from the École des Beaux-Arts, others from American architects of national reputation. Also, fund raising was begun for an endowment of a traveling fellowship, preferably for the study of European ecclesiastical architecture.

Adelsperger developed further the design curriculum that Schlacks and Ackerman had set up. Calling it "The Beaux-Arts Course," it aimed to give students a systematic and thorough training in architectural design and composition, along with a practical working knowledge of construction. It was built around work in the studio, based on the French system. The work began in the first year with a study of the orders and simple problems involving their combination and use and continued over the following three years by means of problems involving the planning of various types of buildings from the simplest to the most monumental. It was supplemented by exercises in the methods and media of rendering.[38]

Notre Dame's curriculum followed directly the system that had long been established at MIT and Columbia University, the latter of which had just opened two new studio classes under the direction of Beaux-Arts-trained Charles Follen McKim and Thomas Hastings. There the students' designs were judged competitively by a jury consisting of the studio heads and other practicing architects in New York. The juries awarded "passes," "mentions" and "special mentions," each of which gave the students a certain number of credits toward their course requirements.[39] While South Bend couldn't offer jurors like Charles McKim or Thomas Hastings, Notre Dame's method of teaching nevertheless put it on a par with what was occurring in the east coast schools, those institutions that have always considered themselves to be the leaders in architectural education. But even here such judgments are relative, for William Ware himself publically lamented in 1898 that MIT couldn't match the quality of faculty at the École des Beaux-Arts, the opportunity for personal guidance by the best French architects:

> This advantage a school like our own cannot possess. It must be carried on not by exceptional men occupying conspicuous positions in the ranks of the profession, but by ordinary persons like ourselves, fairly intelligent and well-informed, but who, however devoted and faithful are nothing out of the common.[40]

The architectural engineering courses in the newly designated college at Notre Dame provided a balance throughout the curriculum's four years by emphasizing the more practical issues of materials, methods of building and structural design. Lessons were supplemented by frequent inspection trips to important construction sites in South Bend and on the University grounds. They also included the writing of specifications and practical work in the trades so the students would be able to superintend construction intelligently. Standard handbooks and millbooks were used as textbooks. Further, graphic methods of determining stresses in beams, girders and trusses were studied and numerous practical problems solved, although it was assumed that for any difficult structural problems the architect would consult an engineer. The technical aspects of building have always been strongly emphasized in the department, something typical of a more pragmatic rather than ideological approach, a characteristic of the Midwestern schools in general.

I n 1909, a new member of the faculty, Francis Wynn Kervick, brought increased impetus to the Beaux-Arts curriculum. A graduate of the University of Pennsylvania — like MIT, Columbia and Harvard, an ardent proponent of the French system — he had such a great interest in France that he soon took a year's leave to work in Paris, where he absorbed firsthand the Beaux-Arts method of design and education. When he returned to South Bend, he maintained the Beaux-Arts system for the next 35 years, with course work centered around the studio, and all instruction in planning and composition being based on what were described in the University *Bulletin* as "accepted principles of design," namely European and classical.[41]

The wave of classicism that predominated both in the profession and the classroom during the first years of the 20th century manifested itself architecturally on the Notre Dame campus in 1917 with the construction of the University Library, now Bond Hall and home of the School of Architecture. Designed by New York architect Edward Tilton, it was the only building to be constructed on the campus in such an overt neoclassical style. Further, it was built with walls of Bedford limestone rather than the yellow brick that was common to the campus at the time. It featured a classical entrance porch with Ionic columns and rows of round-arched windows that illuminated high-ceilinged reading rooms in a manner similar to the Boston Public Library and the Bibliothèque Sainte-Geneviève in Paris.

Edward Tilton was among the leaders of the profession working in the classical style in the 1920s, a cadre of largely east coast architects that included McKim, Mead and White, John Russell Pope, Charles Platt and Henry Bacon. In Chicago there was Graham, Anderson, Probst and White, a large firm that inherited much of the practice of Daniel Burnham and had to their credit the Wrigley Building, the Federal Reserve Bank Building, Union Station and the Straus Building. One of the partners, Ernest Graham, had attended Notre Dame in the years before its architecture program was

Figure 10.
Francis Wynn Kervick

Figure 11.
Paul Anthony Rigali. A Greek Doric Hexastyle-Peripteral Temple. Mention, Beaux-Arts Institute of Design Department of Architecture Archaeology IV Projet, 1933.

officially established; but the most gifted partner was Peirce Anderson, a graduate of the École des Beaux-Arts, who had been instrumental in producing Burnham's city plans for Baguio and Manila in the Philippines.[42] Such firms had all the most important commissions in the country, and they had a great influence on most of the country's university administrators and boards of trustees, a fact which led to innumerable planning schemes for campus development, all in keeping with the principles and character of the City Beautiful Movement.[43]

In 1931 Graham, Anderson, Probst and White designed the Notre Dame College of Commerce, a large and centrally located structure sited in order to define one corner of the campus's main quad and enhance its overall cross-axial plan. The College of Commerce is also notable for the fact that it represented a high point on the campus for the neo-Gothic style, which was long the major rival of classicism for university and ecclesiastical architecture. The work of James Gamble Rogers on the campuses of Yale and Northwestern universities, for instance, were among the most important collegiate Gothic buildings of the period. On the Notre Dame campus in the early 1920s, Francis Kervick along with another faculty member, Vincent Fagan, designed several buildings, all in an elegant and economical Gothic style. Their first project, in 1922, was the addition of the Memorial Porch to Basilica of the Sacred Heart. Shortly afterward they were the associated architects with the New York firm of Cram and Ferguson to build the South Dining Hall, and they designed the complex of dormitories consisting of Howard, Morrissey and Lyons halls. In 1933 Kervick also designed the Engineering Building, Cushing Hall, which was his largest and most successful commission.[44]

After acting as head of the program for six years, Kervick officially assumed the chairmanship in 1920.[45] However, like many others in the country, Notre Dame's College of Architecture suffered severe cutbacks in the period immediately after World War I. The early 1920s was a time of both cultural crisis and a recession in the building professions, and the administration took drastic steps — probably premature given the unprecedented building boom that occurred later in the decade — by reversing many of the ambitious changes made by Rolland Adelsperger, beginning with the change from an independent College of Architecture to a department within the College of Engineering, and the termination of the master's degree program.

By the late 1920s, as enrollment started to increase and the building industry was revived, Kervick took the initiative to enrich the department's training in classical design by participating in the New York-based Beaux-Arts Institute of Design (BAID),

Figure 12.
The Architects' Club on the Administration Building steps, 1911. Francis Kervick and Rolland Adelsperger are first and second from the left, front row.

which sent out design programs to universities across the country, and then judged the students' work on a competitive basis. The BAID had been founded by several architects including Lloyd Warren, a graduate of the École des Beaux-Arts and a sort of 20th-century equivalent to Richard Morris Hunt as an architectural educator. The type of interschool competition initiated by the BAID program tended to raise the standards of architectural education in the United States as a whole.[46] At Notre Dame, *analytiques* issued by the BAID were used principally in the first and second years, often in conjunction with sketch problems written by the faculty.[47] In the 1930s, BAID programs were used throughout the curriculum, with an initial judging by a local jury, and the winners being then submitted to New York.

During the Depression years, though the building industry collapsed, enrollment in architecture remained steady. A new faculty member was even added in 1933, John E. Miller, a graduate of the Catholic University of America. The students at this time took more electives: French, English and art in the first and second years, and philosophy and art in the third year. The undergraduate degree program was also changed from four to five years following a general trend among undergraduate schools in the country. In conjunction with this change, the thesis project was expanded to include an original problem selected with the approval of the faculty and developed by the students, with design, details and structural drawings being required.[48]

Throughout the 1930s, the design curriculum continued to be complemented by courses in the history of architecture. According to a statement in the 1939 *Bulletin,* the classes in the history of architecture were considered highly important, because history offered so much material for illustrations of past achievements and of current problems. Related to studies in architectural history were the history of civilization, the development of painting and sculpture, and studies in philosophy and religion.[49] The basis of the design studio began to change, however, as a dissatisfaction began to settle in among schools across the country. As Fikret Yegül explains, while students produced

Figure 13.

The Architects' Club, 1918. Francis Kervick is seated third from the right. His future partner, Vincent Fagan, is seated far right.

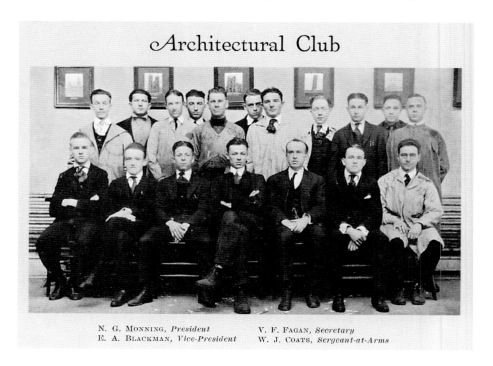

eArchitectural Club

N. G. MONNING, *President*   V. F. FAGAN, *Secretary*
E. A. BLACKMAN, *Vice-President*   W. J. COATS, *Sergeant-at-Arms*

the most monumental schemes imaginable in a florid and grandiose manner, the realization was dawning that such projects were absurdly unrelated to the economic and social conditions brought about by the Depression.[50] New ideas began to take hold through the influence of European modernism, the Bauhaus, and more directly the International Style Exhibition at the Museum of Modern Art in 1932 and the publication of Johnson and Hitchcock's *International Style.* Even so, the transition to outright modernism, especially in the schools of the Midwest, was a very slow process.

The person who most enthusiastically and single-handedly led the school through the transition to modernism was Frank Montana, who joined the faculty as an instructor in 1939. He had received a bachelor of architecture degree from New York University, earned a diploma from the Beaux-Arts Institute of Design in New York, and had won the Paris Prize in 1936. This allowed him to attend the École des Beaux-Arts, where he received a diploma just before beginning his teaching career at Notre Dame.[51] He went on to become chairman of the department in 1950, a position he held until 1972.

Besides his teaching, Montana distinguished himself as an architect, designing the Notre Dame Center for Continuing Education, post office, bookstore and University Club, among other University commissions undertaken with his partner Robert J. Schultz. In Jerusalem, he worked many years for Notre Dame on the buildings of the Ecumenical Institute for Advanced Theological Studies. In South Bend, he also designed the terminal building of the Michiana Regional Airport.

Among Montana's most notable accomplishments within the architecture department were its move in 1964 from Crowley Hall to its present home in the former University Library, and the establishment in 1969 of the Rome Studies Center, which became a required destination for third-year students. He became the director of the Rome Studies Center when he stepped down from the chairmanship in 1972, serving in that post until 1975 and again from 1980 to 1986.

It was during Montana's tenure that the classical and Italian Renaissance styles and the principles of the City Beautiful Movement were gradually replaced by simplified, columnless classicism, which had become popular in public and government buildings and was widely represented in journals. As Yegül points out, the leaders of the classical movement now found themselves in a reactionary position, defending themselves against young architects who defined themselves as new modernists — influenced by the art movements of Expressionism, Futurism and the Bauhaus. However, the acceptance of modernism in the United States in general, and at Notre Dame in particular, was not a sudden event.[52] Montana was a man of very different training and aesthetic taste from his more radical counterparts, Walter Gropius at Harvard and Mies van der Rohe at the Illinois Institute of Technology (IIT). His was a more moderate approach to change. In university architecture schools across the country, the general relaxing of the rules that had required students to follow the classical canon took a long period of time, and was in many cases resisted altogether.[53]

The most influential mode of modernism to affect architecture at Notre Dame in the early years of Montana's tenure was the Art Deco. Receiving a special impetus in the United States after the Exposition Internationale Moderne in Paris in 1925, it was characterized by slender, untapered, squared piers and abstracted capitals, a compositional mode that challenged the basis of the canonical style.[54] While the plans of most buildings designed in this transitional period tended to follow a literal use of Beaux-Arts principles — grandiosity, clear articulation of the parts, balance and hierarchy — their

Figure 14.
Frank Montana

Figure 15.
Ambrose Richardson

Figure 16.
Robert L. Amico

elevations tended more and more to abstraction.[55] The buildings looked modern without losing altogether their grounding in the principles of classicism.

When Montana stepped down as chairman in 1972, he was replaced by Ambrose Richardson, a graduate of IIT and student of Mies van der Rohe, someone more firmly grounded in the modernist movement. Richardson had worked for the Chicago office of Skidmore, Owings and Merrill, where he became a protégé of Nathaniel Owings and an innovator in the development of the International Style. He later established a practice in Champaign, Illinois, where he designed numerous buildings for the University of Illinois during the 1960s and early 1970s, including dormitories and classroom buildings, and the Krannert Art Museum. He is most noted for his design of the Indianapolis Art Museum and, at Notre Dame, the Snite Museum of Art.

Throughout Richardson's tenure as chairman of the department from 1972 to 1978, as in most other schools in the United States, modernism predominated, following closely the current developments in institutional and commercial, especially high-rise, design. The department's reputation for winning competitions was increased, as Notre Dame student Michael A. Manfredi won the Paris Prize competition for the year 1975.[56]

It was also during Richardson's chairmanship, under the presidency of Father Theodore Hesburgh, that the first women were admitted to Notre Dame in 1972. Sixteen women enrolled in the College of Engineering in the first year, but only a handful were in architecture. Within a few years, they typically made up about one-third of the class, a figure that remained more or less constant until the 1990s, when the ratio approached half men and half women. The same cannot be said about the faculty, however. To date, Esmée Bellalta has been the only tenured female faculty member, teaching half-time from 1976 until her retirement in 1995.

Ambrose Richardson was followed by Robert Amico, with Dr. Roger Schmitz serving as dean of the College of Engineering, the two directing the department through the period of the 1980s. Amico held architecture degrees from the University of Illinois at Urbana-Champaign and from Harvard. He had also worked in Chicago for the modernist firm of C.F. Murphy and Associates, and then taught at the University of Illinois before coming to Notre Dame. During Amico's tenure, the department was elevated to the status of a school within the College of Engineering. He also instituted substantial curriculum changes and established the school's first computer laboratory.

Although the school had discontinued its graduate programs in 1919, it established an affiliated program in 1968 that offered a master of environic design. Directed by the British architect Patrick Horsbrugh, this program attracted both American and foreign students interested in issues related to planning and environmental design. In 1985, it was superceded by a new post-professional program leading to the master of architecture degree, with a specialization in urban design.

The school's theoretical approach during Amico's chairmanship followed closely the postmodernist work of architects like Charles Moore, Michael Graves and Richard Meier, focusing both on a return to traditional styles and on the theories of Colin Rowe's urban contextualism. Two faculty members, Norman Crowe and Steven Hurtt, both former students of Rowe at Cornell, brought to Notre Dame an intense interest in urban design that preferred the traditional city over the modern one. Colin Rowe himself made a significant contribution to the school in the mid-1980s when he taught in the Rome Studies Program. His suggestion that the fourth-year curriculum should focus on Chicago — setting up for the students a Rome-Chicago dialogue — was profoundly influential, giving the students a basis for engaging the American city with what they learned in Rome.

D uring this period the University further solidified its support for the Rome Studies Program by purchasing for the school the principal floors of two adjacent palaces in the historic center of the city on Via Monterone. Since the founding of the Rome Studies Program in 1969, it has served as an integral part of the five-year bachelor's degree program. It is the only such yearlong international studies program among American university architecture schools that is required for all its students. With an average enrollment of 40 to 45 students, its faculty is composed of three design instructors, an artist, and two architectural historians. Most importantly, it provides for Notre Dame its greatest advantage over the established east coast schools: the opportunity for all of its students to acquire an in-depth understanding and appreciation of one of the great

European centers for architecture and urbanism, its focus based upon a re-exploration of the language of classical architecture. The understanding of Rome it provides within the school is broad-based, influencing students and faculty alike as a common point of reference.

The design studio of the Rome Studies Program is aimed first of all at introducing the students to the architectural elements that compose the traditional city. They are asked to analyze a quarter of Rome, a piazza, a street, a palace and a church as essential elements of the urban context. They typically begin with a design on the urban scale and work their way down to the scale of a building and a room. In the first project the students are required to analyze a series of piazzas in Rome's historical center and then to relate what they have learned through an urban design project. Sites for projects have included the area around the Mausoleum of Augustus, an undeveloped block on the Via Giulia, the Crypta Balbi and the Forum Boarium. This urban project is followed by a series of projects involving palace-type buildings, churches, housing and other building types, again, each beginning with an analytical assignment that can inform the final design projects within the Roman context. In the spring semester, the students are given projects that include a villa on a suburban site near Rome, one that involves both building and garden design.

Not only is the teaching of classical and Renaissance architecture important to the Notre Dame program, but so too are the principles of traditional urbanism, ones that can best be learned by direct study in Italy. Urban issues are addressed in the history and theory classes — the development of the forum, the piazza, building types, patterns of development, city boundaries, patronage, and social and economic determinants. Term projects in the history classes include reconstruction drawings of ancient or Renaissance buildings and analytical studies of cities and towns. The sketching and watercolor courses concentrate on representing Roman settings in numerous formats and give the students experience with a variety of drawing media.

Figure 18.
Karl A. Krueger. Sant'Ivo della Sapienza, Rome, 1987.

Figure 19.
Frank Montana. Roman Forum, 27 October 1980.

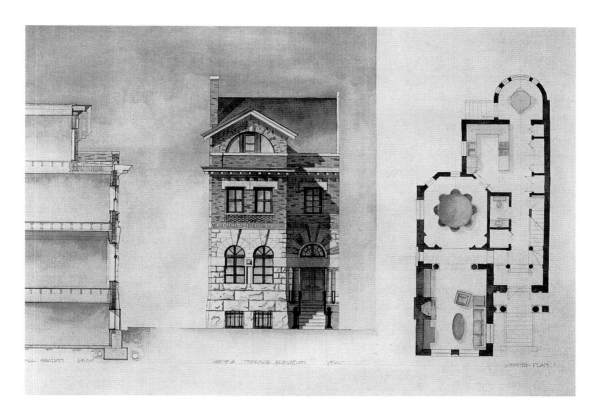

everal changes were initiated in the school in 1989, ones that complemented more fully the presence of the Rome Studies Program, and resulted in the school becoming a center for a revival of interest in traditional classical and Renaissance architecture. In one sense, it was a return to the school's long association with Beaux-Arts classicism and the City Beautiful Movement, though in its initial stages, it was more closely related to the personal scholarly direction of the new chairman, Thomas Gordon Smith. Hired by Anthony Michel, then the dean of the College of Engineering, Smith was a graduate of the University of California at Berkeley with a practice in California and teaching experience at the University of Illinois at Chicago. The principal administrative developments under Smith included the hiring of several new faculty members and technical personnel, the development of the Architecture Advisory Council, the total renovation of the school's building, the development and accreditation of a two-year master of architecture degree with a specialty in classical architecture, and the establishment of the school's complete autonomy from the College of Engineering.

Figure 20.
Dana Gulling. Geneva Terrace, Chicago. Plan, elevation and section, 1997.

Figure 21.
Manuel Damian Samora. West Kemper Street elevation, Chicago, 1997.

An architect whose interests focused on a renaissance of classical architecture and the teaching of fundamental design principles based on the writings of Vitruvius, Smith above all made several changes in the school's curriculum and theoretical focus. As Leon Krier suggests, the eradication of the teaching of classical architecture from the profession during the modernist period did not necessarily eliminate the need for it, and thus it was the purpose of Smith's program to explore how the rules of classical architecture could be applied and reinterpreted in today's world.[57]

Figure 22.
Andrea Emilia Peschel.
Slovak Cultural and
Spiritual Center,
Minneapolis, Minnesota.
Site plan, 1997.

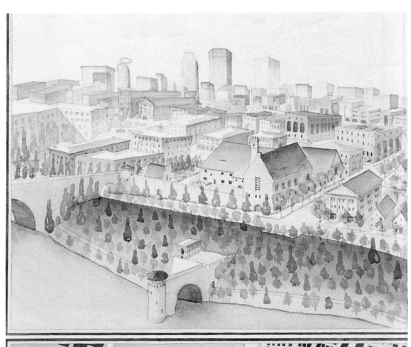

While pluralism has been a much-talked-about trend in architectural education and practice, in fact, modernism remains the dominant force in most schools. As Smith pointed out, most education and practice is based upon the principle of abstraction rather than literal translation, the resulting theory and architecture invariably leading toward minimalism, fragmentation and alienation.[58] Believing that a pluralistic attitude should include a rational way of learning from traditional architecture, not as a point of departure for modernism but as a basis for a continuum of tradition that relies on conviction and principle, Notre Dame's architecture program under Smith was transformed in order to offer an alternative approach to the type of education that has prevailed in other schools since the 1940s.

The commitment thus expected of Notre Dame students is to engage in a discourse with the classical architectural language. It is not a methodology that can be learned easily. It requires a facility with traditional drawing methods, especially ink wash on watercolor paper, the ability to draw the orders, and the firsthand study of ancient and Renaissance monuments. Arguing that classical architecture is the closest to a universal language of architecture, Smith believed it is essential to learn that language well, and that once learned, students would have the best possible basis for developing their own creativity. The classical teaching of Notre Dame's School of Architecture does not simply reduce the past cultures of ancient, Renaissance and baroque Europe to catalogs of available form-works. Instead it is based on an understanding of their timeless principles and techniques through a series of analytical and design studies that involve a practical handling of issues of typology, function, material and context. The intention is not a dogmatic imitation but rather to inspire a respect of tradition that can serve students well in a world that often ignores both respect and tradition.

As the School of Architecture moves toward the 21st century, with its new chairman, Carroll William Westfall, at the helm, it will continue its strong foundation of traditional education and design values while forming closer links to contemporary architectural movements and building practices. Its long interest in the traditional city, Vitruvius, the Beaux-Arts and the City Beautiful Movement, and its substantial reputation as a center of classical studies will serve it well in its response to future developments.

■ ■ ■

ENDNOTES

1. Andrew Saint, "The Building Art of the First Industrial Metropolis," in *London — World City: 1800–1840,* ed. Celina Fox (New Haven and London: Yale University Press in association with the Museum of London, 1992), 59–61.
2. Quoted in John Barrington Bayley and Henry Hope Reed, "Introductory Notes for the Classical American Edition," in William Ware, *The American Vignola* (New York: W.W. Norton, 1977), xi.
3. Michael J. Lewis, "Activism and Architecture: A Tale of Two Cities," *The New Criterion* 16 (June 1998): 85. For information on the École des Beaux-Arts see *The Architecture of the École des Beaux-Arts,* ed. Arthur A. Drexler (New York: Museum of Modern Art, 1977).

4.   Theodor K. Rohdenburg, *A History of the School of Architecture, Columbia University* (New York: Columbia University Press, 1954), 4–5.

5.   Among those who apprenticed in Hunt's office were Henry Van Brunt, William Ware, Charles D. Gambrill, George B. Post and Frank Furness, to name only a few.

6.   Bayley and Reed, "Introductory Notes for the Classical American Edition," xi. Hunt's library collection is now held in the American Institute of Architects Library and Archives in Washington, D.C.

7.   Rohdenburg, *A History of the School of Architecture,* 4, 15; and *The Architect at Mid-Century: Evolution and Achievement,* ed. Turpin Bannister (New York: Reinhold Publishing Corporation, 1954), 96–97.

8.   William A. Coles, "William R. Ware," in *Macmillan Encyclopedia of Architects,* vol. 4, ed. Adolf K. Placzek (New York: The Free Press; London: Collier Macmillan Publishers, 1982), 373–74.

9.   Ware had studied engineering and mathematics at Harvard's Lawrence Scientific Institute and then apprenticed in the New York office of Richard Morris Hunt. Bayley and Reed, "Introductory Notes for the Classical American Edition," ix.

10.   Bayley and Reed, "Introductory Notes for the Classical American Edition," xi.

11.   Coles, "William R. Ware," 374.

12.   Bannister, *The Architect at Mid-Century,* 97; and Wayne Charney and John W. Stamper, "Nathan Clifford Ricker and the Beginnings of Architectural Education in Illinois," Illinois Historical Journal (Winter 1986), 257–260.

13.   Bannister, *The Architect at Mid-Century,* 97.

14.   Ibid., 97–98.

15.   Fiske Kimball, introduction to *The Foundations of Classic Architecture,* by Herbert Langford Warren (New York: MacMillan Company, 1919), vii.

16.   Bannister, *The Architect at Mid-Century,* 98.

17.   Henry Van Brunt, "Architecture at the World's Columbian Exposition," *Century Magazine* 44 (1892): 88.

18.   Charles Mulford Robinson, "Improvement in City Life: Aesthetic Progress," *Atlantic Monthly* 83 (June 1899): 77.

19.   Charles Moore, Daniel H. Burnham (Boston: Houghton Mifflin Co., 1921), vii; and Reid Badger, *The Great American Fair: The World's Columbian Exposition & American Culture* (Chicago: N. Hall, 1979), 115.

20.   William H. Wilson, "J. Horace McFarland and the City Beautiful Movement," *Journal of Urban History* 7 (May 1981): 315–34.

21.   A.D.F. Hamlin, "Twenty-Five Years of American Architecture," *Architectural Record* 40 (July 1916): 8.

22.   Thomas Schlereth, *The University of Notre Dame: A Portrait of its History and Campus* (Notre Dame: University of Notre Dame Press, 1976), 83, 108–109. The College of Engineering had been established as part of the University's science program in 1873. That same year, the college instituted courses in civil engineering, again, the first Catholic university in the country to do so. Mechanical engineering courses added in 1886 and electrical engineering classes in 1891. See Anne Klimek, *The Zahms' Legacy: A History of Engineering at Notre Dame 1873–1993* (Notre Dame: University of Notre Dame College of Engineering, 1993) for a full account.

23.   *Bulletin of the University of Notre Dame* (1904–5), 6.

24.   Ibid., 3–4.

25.   Francis W. Kervick, *Architecture at Notre Dame: A Review to Commemorate the 40th Anniversary of the Department of Architecture, 1898–1938* (Notre Dame: University of Notre Dame, 1938), 4.

26.   *Bulletin of the University of Notre Dame* (1903–4), 8. For more information on Henry Schlacks and his work, see Francis Kervick, *Architects in America of Catholic Tradition* (Rutland, Vt.: C.E. Tuttle Co., 1962), 118, 121, and his own books, *Some Works of Henry J. Schlacks, Architect* (Chicago: Barnes-Crosby Co., 1908) and *The Work of Henry John Schlacks, Ecclesiologist* (Chicago: Press of the Henneberry Co., 1903).

27. Fikret K. Yegül, *Gentlemen of Instinct and Breeding: Architecture at the American Academy in Rome, 1894–1940* (New York: Oxford University Press, 1991), 112–113.

28. *Catalogue of the University of Notre Dame* (1898–99), 65; and *The New World* (14 April 1900), 4.

29. Yegül, *Gentlemen of Instinct,* 3.

30. Herbert Landford Warren, "The Influence of France upon American Architecture," *American Architect and Building News* 66 (25 November 1899): 68.

31. Sergio Villari, *J.N.L. Durand (1760–1834): Art and Science of Architecture,* trans. Eli Gottlieb (New York: Rizzoli International, 1990), 53–55.

32. Alberto Pérez-Gómez, *Architecture and the Crisis of Modern Science* (Cambridge, Mass.: MIT Press, 1983), 313–314.

33. *Catalogue of the University of Notre Dame* (1898–99), 68.

34. Kervick, *Architecture at Notre Dame,* n.p. For more information on Rayneri and the Capitolio, see Carlos Miguel de Céspedes, Republica de Cuba. *Capitolio* (La Habana: Talleres tip. de P. Fernández y compañía, 1933) 730 p.

35. Although Adelsperger did not receive his bachelor of science in architecture from Notre Dame until 1908, he held a bachelor of arts (N.D. 1890) and had served in 1900–1901 as architect for the Department of Charities and Hospitals of the Military Government of the Island of Cuba. He also took the courses at the Armour Institute of Technology and the Art Institute of Chicago School of Architecture. (University Archives, file MDE 1.017)

36. *Bulletin of the University of Notre Dame* (1905–6), 36, 38.

37. Ibid., 72.

38. Ibid., 36.

39. Rohdenburg, *A History of the School of Architecture,* 20.

40. William R. Ware, "The Columbia University School of Architecture," *American Architect and Building News* 61 (6 August 1898): 45.

41. *Bulletin of the University of Notre Dame* (1912), 96–97.

42. John W. Stamper, *Chicago's North Michigan Avenue: Planning and Development, 1900–1930* (Chicago: University of Chicago Press, 1991), 35.

43. Yegül, *Gentlemen of Instinct,* 109.

44. Kervick, *Architecture at Notre Dame;* and Schlereth, *The University of Notre Dame,* 140.

45. Besides Kervick, other members of the faculty in the 1920s included his professional partner Vincent Fagan, who received his bachelor's degree from Notre Dame in 1920, and Brother Ferdinand Moser, C.S.C., a 1923 Notre Dame architecture graduate. Kervick taught not only design but also classes in working drawings, architectural history, decorative arts, and, on occasion, even mechanical systems. Francis Xavier Ackerman still taught mechanical drawing. In 1925, Gerald C. Brubaker, a 1922 Notre Dame graduate, was added to the staff to teach mechanical engineering. *Bulletin of the University of Notre Dame* (1920–21 and 1925–26).

46. Bannister, *The Architect at Mid-Century,* 101.

47. *Official Bulletin of the University of Notre Dame* (1934), 248.

48. *Official Bulletin of the University of Notre Dame* (1935), 264–66.

49. Ibid., 290.

50. Yegül, *Gentlemen of Instinct,* 114.

51. *Official Bulletin of the University of Notre Dame* (1939), 290.

52. Yegül, *Gentlemen of Instinct,* 101, 109.

53. Ibid., 115.

54. Ibid., 86.

55. Ibid., 101.

56. National Institute for Architectural Education, *Yearbook* 53 (1975): 20–21.

57. Leon Krier, forward to *New Classicism: Omnibus Volume,* ed. Andreas Papadakis and Harriet Watson (London: Academy Editions, 1990), 6–7.

58. Thomas Gordon Smith, "Order and Type," in *Building Classical: A Vision of Europe and America,* ed. Richard Economakis (London: Academy Editions, 1993), 189–190.

Figure 23.
A drawing class, 1953.

Housing the Architects:

From the Dome to Bond Hall

■ ■ ■

NORMAN A. CROWE

The design of a building to house teaching programs in architecture is always an intriguing subject. No other architectural design is likely to be more elaborately self-conscious and more exten-sively scrutinized once it is built than a building intended to facilitate teaching students how to design buildings. The history of the design of buildings to house schools of architecture might be characterized as traversing a scale, at one end of which is the intention to create a great work of architecture, overtly monumental, historic and grand, while at the other end is the more recent tendency to create a kind of shop for teaching architecture — its efficient, no-nonsense demeanor expressive of the latest technological means to achieve timely progress.

Standing somewhat outside this scale from the grand to the apparently practical are all those buildings which house schools of architecture that were originally designed for other purposes, their first tenants now gone and instructional programs for architecture settled in their place. If the building's former function was as a warehouse or laboratory, the expression of shoplike efficiency is more likely to be in evidence, while if it was a Beaux-Arts style library as at Notre Dame, the approach will more likely seek to emphasize the embodied memories of timeless values traditionally regarded as intrinsic to classicism. Notre Dame has never had to face the problem of selecting the primary expression for the buildings that housed its programs in architecture, because they had never been the first tenant here. On the other hand, the School of Architecture has had the good fortune to always find itself within one or another of the finest buildings on the campus, as it does now in the newly renovated Bond Hall.

Academic programs in architecture at Notre Dame have been housed in four places on the campus and two in Rome. Architecture began on the Notre Dame campus in 1898 on the fifth floor of the Administration Building, now the Main Building or more popularly known as "The Dome," where it remained until 1931 when it moved from there into the building known today as Crowley Hall. Then in 1964, the school moved from Crowley Hall to the

Figure 24.
**The Administration
Building, c1900.**

former campus library after the University's library collection had been relocated to the newly completed Memorial Library. The school has remained in the former Lemonnier Library since 1964, with the exception of a year and a half when it occupied the former quarters of the College of Business Administration's Hayes-Healy and Hurley complex, in 1996 and 1997, while the Architecture Building underwent extensive renovation. As for the Rome Studies Program, facilities adequate to accommodate a full-year teaching program began in rented quarters on the outskirts of the city but were soon moved to its present location on the Via Monterone in the old *Centro Storico* in 1969. These quarters were purchased in 1985 by the University and subsequently renovated.

While Architecture at Notre Dame has never been housed in a building designed for it from the onset, places selected for it, with the exception of its brief stay in Hayes-Healy and Hurley, have provided plenty of open and unobstructed space for the studios that serve as drafting rooms, a particular requirement for the teaching of architecture. The studio, which is at the heart of the teaching program, requires good natural lighting and plenty of flexibility in arrangement to accommodate a variety of functions and class sizes. In addition to the studios are requirements for classrooms, administrative and faculty offices and library accommodations, all similar or identical to that of other disciplines and programs on campus. A further "requirement" of Architecture, however — one that is not so easily described — involves being housed within a building that is worthy of comparison with the inevitable array of philosophical arguments that characterize the art and science of architecture. This intrinsic characteristic of the discipline of architecture leads to its inclusion in facilities that are themselves architecturally refined to the extent they may be seen by students and faculty as reflecting in one way or another many of the values architects strive to engage. The Main Building, Crowley Hall, the Lemonnier Library and the building that houses the Rome Studies Program — all fine buildings in the first place — satisfy this requirement very well. In an academic setting, architecture is charged with a responsibility for teaching technological proficiency, but because architecture is also understood as a cultural entity, the expressive qualities and, ultimately, cultural reflections manifested in the place where it is taught are just as important to faculty and students as functional considerations.

The first home of the School of Architecture, on the top floor of the Main Building, placed studios, library and classrooms within the generous open space beneath its trussed roof. Architecture shared the top floor with a fine arts program, considered an allied discipline and which required similar spatial accommodations in the form of studios. The Main Building, the third of the three buildings to occupy that site, had been built almost in its entirety in several months after the destruction of its predecessor by fire in April 1879. Its architect, Willoughby J. Edbrooke of Chicago, referred to the stylistic character of the new building as "modern Gothic."[1] For Architecture, the fifth floor of the Main Building provided large rooms that were one-and-a-half stories in height, part of a largely free-plan interior — that is, freestanding columns rather than intermediate bearing walls, thereby allowing larger aggregate and thus more flexible spaces beneath the roof. Furthermore, due to the fact that the top floor of the Main Building was actually within the roof structure, the rooms yielded a sloping ceiling at the outside walls and a series of secondary spaces created by the many dormers. This provided for a more interesting spatial experience than would be the case with a purely flat ceiling of a rectangular room. In addition, this location provided sky lighting at the centers of the larger spaces, offering diffused light so important to studio use, especially before the refinement of broad general ambient lighting by means of electrical fixtures.

By 1931 Architecture had outgrown its accommodations in the Main Building. Hoynes Hall, today known as the Patrick F. Crowley Hall of Music, became available at this time and chairman Francis Kervick moved the program into it after relatively minimal interior remodeling. Hoynes Hall was built in 1919 from the shell of a building that had housed the Institute of Technology. That building had burned in 1916 and was rebuilt in 1919 to become the Law School and was named Hoynes Hall for a flamboyant dean and professor of law at Notre Dame for over 50 years. The designer of the reconstruction was Brother Columbkille, C.S.C. His design accommodated a moot court on the main floor, a law library, and classrooms and offices suited to their particular purposes throughout the building. In 1930, the renovation for Architecture

Figure 25.
The Architecture Building (now Crowley Hall of Music), c1920.

27

involved modification of the interior by the removal of partitions on the second floor where it was structurally possible to do so, thereby providing relatively unrestricted spaces for studios. When completed, the remodeling accommodated two generous studios on the second floor and a library of 800 volumes on the first floor. Also on the first floor was a lecture room with a projection lantern for the school's collection of glass-mounted slides. The large arched windows of that building provided generous natural lighting for the deep interior spaces as required by Architecture's studios, and its basic neo-Renaissance proportions instilled the building with a classical character, in contrast to the neo-Gothic and Victorian and the rather vernacular version of French Second Empire architecture evident across most of the rest of the campus.

In 1964, having outgrown its quarters despite an extension built in 1947, the school moved into the former campus library building. The move came after the University's library collection had moved to the new Memorial Library, known today as the Hesburgh Library. Interestingly, a number of schools of architecture across the country reside in former campus libraries. Their large open interiors intended for circulation, stacks and reading rooms provide ideal spaces for architecture studios and review and exhibition rooms. Further, the customary architectural quality and detailed refinement of campus libraries tends to invite the attention of architects. In the case of the building that eventually came to house Notre Dame's School of Architecture, the numbers and timing work out almost magically. The building's first dedication, that is as the Lemonnier Library, took place on June 3, 1917, and served as a centerpiece for the celebration of the University's Diamond Jubilee. The recent renovation, which began in the summer of 1995 and was completed in January 1997, occurred just a year before the School of Architecture at Notre Dame turns 100. In other words, Bond Hall turned 80 in 1997, having been built in the first place as part of the University's 75th anniversary celebration, and in 1998 the newly dedicated building accommodated the School of Architecture during its 100th year at Notre Dame.

The first renovation of the campus library for use by Architecture was guided by then-chairman of the School of Architecture Frank Montana who had convinced the University to turn the former library over to the School and whose skill as an architect provided very workable quarters for the program, in spite of tight budget constraints at the time. The building's name was changed from the Lemonnier Library to the Architecture Building, and the program set up operations within it when classes began in the fall of 1964. The very extensive renovation accomplished more recently was

Figure 26.
Inauguration of the renovated Lemonnier Library building: Pietro Belluschi, Rev. Theodore Hesburgh, C.S.C., dean of engineering Norman Gay and Frank Montana, 1 May 1965.

Figure 27.
Foyer of the Architecture Building, c1969.

completed in 1996, and the rededication of the building, this time renamed Bond Hall of Architecture, took place on March 21, 1997. The dedication involved two-and-a-half days of events that included the blessing of the building by University president Rev. Edward Malloy, C.S.C., as well as a series of events attended by the donors, Joanne and William Bond, members of their family, various personages among the University's administration, and the School of Architecture faculty and students. Faculty presented papers on the first afternoon of the celebration, and President Malloy and others addressed faculty, friends and University dignitaries along with the donors and their family at a dinner in the Hesburgh Library that evening.

On the following day, the University awarded honorary doctorates to architects Demetri Porphyrios of London, Allan Greenberg of New York and Washington, D.C., and Elizabeth Plater-Zyberk, architect and dean of the College of Architecture at the University of Miami, Florida. Greenberg and Plater-Zyberk each gave an address in the Snite Museum's Annenberg Auditorium in a convocation during the morning, and Porphyrios gave an address at the conference of honorary degrees in the auditorium during the afternoon. Greenberg is known for his contemporary classical designs in the United States, Porphyrios for his traditional and classical work in Europe, America and the Near East, as well as for theoretical writings published worldwide, and Plater-Zyberk for her work as part of what has come to be known as the New Urbanism Movement, led by her Miami firm of Duany and Plater-Zyberk.

The architect of record for the extensive renovation of Bond Hall was campus architect Ellerbe-Becket Associates, with the chairman of the School of Architecture, Thomas Gordon Smith, as principal designer. The original 1917 building is by New York architect Edward Tilton, who had established a sound reputation as a specialist in library design with numerous town libraries for the Carnegie Foundation as well as other university libraries to his credit. The new library broke with tradition at Notre Dame, becoming the first and still the only example of full-fledged Beaux-Arts inspired Renaissance classicism on the campus. Tilton was trained in the offices of McKim, Mead and White of New York. Another notable building by architects McKim, Mead and White was Robinson Hall, which housed Harvard's School of Architecture. Before working with that firm, Tilton had attended the École des Beaux-Arts in Paris. He opened his practice in 1890 and, when contacted by Notre Dame in 1915, had just

Figure 28.
Rev. Edward Malloy, C.S.C., and chairman Thomas Gordon Smith with benefactors William and Joanne Bond, 21 March 1997.

Figure 29.
Honorary degree recipients Demetri Porphyrios, Elizabeth Plater-Zyberk and Allan Greenberg.

completed a library in Springfield, Massachusetts, that was inspired by McKim, Mead and White's internationally known Boston Public Library of 1894.

Preliminary to accepting the commission from Notre Dame, Tilton wrote that "The building's dress should be graceful but not excessive of its functions and explanatory of its raison d'être, not concealing its biblio muscles and arteries by too much overskirt."[2] While that would sound like the bare bones of exposed structure and mechanical equipment by today's standards, to Tilton it meant a building of appropriately dignified neo-Renaissance classical form and detail, durable materials and an efficient internal organization to facilitate its designated functions without extreme elaboration of decorative detail as had become so typical of neo-baroque architecture of that time.

Placement of the new library was to be at the head of a proposed "academic quadrangle" that was envisioned by the third head of the school, Francis Wynn Kervick, in his long-range campus plan proposal that reached its final form in 1920. Kervick must surely have seen the strong bilateral symmetry and commanding facade of the new library as appropriate to a building that would preside over a new quadrangle in concert with the symbolic importance of a campus library. While his scheme for an academic quadrangle remained unrealized, thereby relegating the campus library to an uncharacteristically inauspicious position for a building whose role was intended as central to the University, such a secondary position seems perfectly appropriate to its present role of housing a separate academic unit within the University.

Some further comments regarding the design of the original building are in order. The library building was designed at the onset to house considerably more than books. It was designed to accommodate the University's Dante Collection as well as a historical museum and art collection. The library was intended to accommodate an eventual collection of 618,000 volumes in a closed stack system. The final design included seating for 360 readers — one third of the University's enrollment at the time — in two reading rooms, each 108 feet by 32 feet, paralleling the north and south side elevations of the building and flanking the circulation lobby and public foyer that lay at the center. There were five decks of closed stacks supported by a cast-iron commercial prefabricated library stack system and serviced from the central circulation desk, with the card catalog at the very center of the building under a grand skylight. The Dante Collection, historical museum and art collection were housed in rooms on the top floor of the building along the north, west and south sides. The stacks were placed between the reading rooms and the circulation center, supported by the cast-iron stack system that extended from the basement to just below the top floor. The relatively newly available application of electric lighting for library stacks allowed this part of the building to be isolated from exterior walls and thus from natural light.[3]

Figure 30.
The Lemonnier Library card catalog room, c1960.

The structure of the building itself consists of a cast-in-place concrete frame with
structural clay tile infilling the interstices of the frame, the whole clad on the exterior
with grey Indiana limestone and the interior with plaster. The main public spaces
(foyer, lobby and central circulation) were rendered in plaster, but here plaster surfaces
yielded an ensemble of classical moldings and pilasters as well as paneled divisions of
the more expansive surfaces. Classical details throughout these public spaces followed
closely the drawings and instructions published in the popular handbook for classical
detailing known as *The American Vitruvius*, available to designers and builders since
1902. Elsewhere the plaster walls were smooth and unarticulated, while doors,
windows, and their frames were of oak, varnished over a warm-toned stain. A rich
green terra-cotta tile was selected for the roof, which skirted the perimeter of the
building, leaving a T-shaped well over the two-story-high lobby and central "courtyard," with skylights positioned over the foyer and the circulation "courtyard" spaces.
Floors in the major public spaces, including the museum rooms on the top floor and
even the walkways between rows of book stacks were laid out in grey Vermont
marble.

The *parti* for the building itself (that is, its basic architectural organization) is based
on the Italian palazzo, with the palazzo's characteristic courtyard, or *cortile*, at the
center, now skylit as an interior court. The triumphal arch at the entrance was the first
in a succession of five arches that led to the skylit court and beyond, setting up a motif
of arched openings to be repeated in the large arched windows on east, north and
south elevations. The arched windows across the facade, with their two smaller
rectangular companion windows below, recall familiar libraries of the past, especially
the Bibliothèque Sainte-Geneviève in Paris and McKim, Mead and White's Boston
Public Library, which faces Copley Square. The high arched windows on both sides of
the building lit the two reading rooms, without the two smaller windows below them
on these elevations so as not to undercut the monumentality of the more important
east facade.

Figure 31.
Bond Hall before the
renovation.

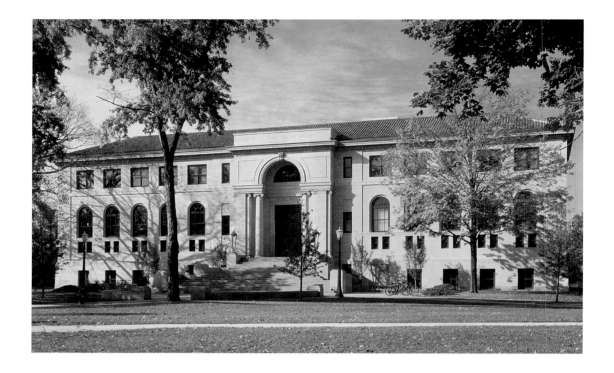

Figures 32 and 33.
Bond Hall after the addition and renovation, fall 1997.

The 1995–97 renovation of the building left the exterior essentially unchanged except for cleaning and restoration on the facade and side elevations. It included an addition to the rear of the building to accommodate two stair shafts, an elevator, and a small amount of additional space for design studios for the graduate program, four seminar-presentation rooms, and the Architecture Library's new rare books room. The exterior monumental stairway in the front was renovated, but its basic form today recalls the spirit and form of the original. The interior, however, is extensively changed, with the Architecture Library now occupying the former *cortile* at the center, as well as expanding into the former gallery and stack spaces that surround the central "courtyard" space. The floor of the lobby-foyer is terrazzo where it was once grey Vermont marble, and the *cortile,* now the circulation area for the library, was designed by Thomas Gordon Smith as a Doric peristyle beneath a new skylight, the arches that once graced the front and back wall of that space now removed. The former reading rooms of the Lemonnier Library (flanking spaces on the north and south sides of the building) are now subdivided into a 99-seat auditorium and an exhibition gallery on the north side, and administrative offices, a conference room and a classroom on the south side. Most of the studios on the upper level of the building remain, while faculty offices ring most of the outside wall at that level. In addition, there is a studio on what had been the roof where the skylight over the entrance foyer once stood, and there is the addition of an entire floor across much of the middle of the building in the place of the former stacks, thereby considerably expanding the space available for studios. Freshman studios are located on the north side of the ground floor, and sophomore studios on the south side at that same level. Fourth-year studios are above the sophomore studios are on the mezzanine level, and the fifth-year studios are on the top floor. In other words, as students progress through the program in architecture, they move upward level by level within the building. Beneath the seating of the auditorium on the main floor is a café specializing in cappuccino and sandwiches, known as Café Poché, open throughout the week and managed by University Food Services. The basement also includes a new computer cluster in the center-front and an extensively equipped woodshop in the northwest portion. The woodshop accommodates the special needs of a new furniture design program that Robert Brandt began in January 1992.

Figure 34.
In the fourth-year studio, Bond Hall, 1999.

Finally, a mention of specifics of the accommodations for the Rome Center should be made here as well. After all, the Rome facilities are as much a part of the program as is Bond Hall on the main campus. While the School of Architecture had occupied the same building since 1969 as rented quarters, eventual purchase took place in 1985. The building was then renovated and, on January 16, 1986, Rev. Theodore Hesburgh, C.S.C., presided at a dedication ceremony that included Architecture chairman Robert Amico, Rome director Frank Montana, Engineering dean Roger Schmitz and Rome chaplain Rev. Jose Martelli, C.S.C., along with faculty, students and the U.S. ambassador to Italy, Maxwell Rabb. The Rome facilities include studios for about 50 graduate and undergraduate students, administrative offices, a library, a classroom and a computer room all on the second floor, or *piano nobile*, while on the ground floor are a formal exhibition and reception space, an auxiliary small studio or office, and a kitchen and dining area for the students' use in preparing their own meals. The gallery is connected to the second level by a grand stair in white and colored marble. The larger rooms of the second floor boast frescoed ceilings from the 19th century, while the whole of the building dates most likely from the 16th century.

Figure 35.
Rome Studies Center inaugural celebration, 16 January 1986. At the head table are (left to right): Mrs. Ruth Montana, chairman Bob Amico, Mrs. Rabb, Rev. Theodore Hesburgh, C.S.C., ambassador Maxwell Rabb, dean Roger Schmitz, Rome director Frank Montana.

Figure 36.
The Rome Studies Center, Via Monterone, 1999.

To some, moving into buildings designed long ago to serve a purpose they eventually outgrew might carry a stigma not unlike having to accept an older sibling's hand-me-downs. That is a particularly modern way of looking at things — to presume something old to be outmoded. A work of architecture, however, especially when it is a fine and durable building from the onset, may improve with age. "Improve" in this instance does not necessarily imply functional considerations; it has instead to do with a sense of the past in the present. We often associate events with places and things we think of as permanent, and buildings of quality often become rich vehicles for the conveyance of memories. The 19th-century French architect and pedagogue Auguste Choisy said that "buildings classify themselves as witnesses fixing the way of life and the moral condition of humanity, age by age."[4] He was reflecting on a time when the fabric of cities was seen as synonymous with the fabric of civilization, when memory was embodied in the architecture of a place as much as in its libraries, museums and archives. Bond Hall and the Via Monterone properties are inextricably tied to the history of Notre Dame and Rome.

The philosophy of the School of Architecture includes a strong respect for traditional and classical architecture as well as traditional approaches to urban design. Concomitant with an understanding and concern for traditional and classical design, the school advocates the continued development of environmentally sensitive approaches to design. A part of the faculty's wish to remain in the building that Architecture has occupied since 1964, as opposed to constructing a new building somewhere else on the campus, had to do with a concern for the conservation of resources — both natural and cultural. While the renovation of an existing building preserves materials already prepared, extending its life extends its capacity to evoke associations with the past. We like to think of Bond Hall and the Rome campus as set for many more years of service to the University and to the School of Architecture, representing a tangible link between our past and our future.

■ ■ ■

ENDNOTES

1. Quoted in Thomas J. Schlereth, *The University of Notre Dame: A Portrait of Its History and Campus* (Notre Dame: University of Notre Dame Press, 1976), 58.
2. Edward L. Tilton, "Architecture of Small Libraries," *Public Libraries* 17 (February 1912): 40.
3. Marsha Stevenson, "Style and Symbol: Library Buildings at Notre Dame" in *What is Written Remains: Historical Essays on the Libraries of Notre Dame*, ed. Maureen Gleason and Katharina J. Blackstead (Notre Dame: University of Notre Dame Press, 1994), 194–96.
4. Auguste Choisy, *Histoire de l'architecture* (Paris, 1899), 1:14; quoted in Reyner Banham, *Theory and Design in the First Machine Age*, 2nd ed. (New York: Praeger, 1967), 26.

Figure 37.
The Architects' Club on the Administration Building steps,
1920. Vincent Fagan is seated front row left.

Figure 38.
The Architects' Club outside the Rockne Memorial, 1949.

The Golden Chain:

The Kervick-Montana Years

■ ■ ■

DENNIS P. DOORDAN

The centenary of an educational program is an occasion for celebration. It is also an opportunity to reflect upon the past. How does a school of architecture change? How does a small, university-based design program in northern Indiana engage the national issues and concerns of professional practitioners? What insights into 20th-century American architecture can be gained by examining the experience of one educational program? Other essays in this volume offer panoramic surveys of a century of architectural education at Notre Dame. This essay serves as a case study of the architecture program at midcentury, a moment that corresponds roughly to the midpoint of the Notre Dame program's own history and marked an important transition in the department's leadership. In 1950, Frank Montana succeeded Francis Kervick as chairman of the Department of Architecture. Kervick joined the faculty in 1909 and was officially appointed chairman of the department in 1920 (after acting as *de facto* head since 1914). Montana arrived at Notre Dame in 1939, and his tenure as chairman extended from 1950 to 1972. Each man left a significant legacy for Notre Dame, and, together, their terms at the helm of the program constitute over half of the 100-year history of architecture at Notre Dame.

The University's archival holdings of student work from the Kervick-Montana years are regrettably sparse, but two surviving and documented student projects provide a "snapshot" view of the past suggestive of the spectrum of design present during this period. A large drawing of an Etruscan Gate produced in 1936 by George Beltemacchi (class of 1936) is testimony to the role of archaeological study in the education of young designers during the Kervick years. Students developed graphic skills and

Figure 39.

George A. Beltemacchi.
An Etruscan Gate. Mention,
Beaux-Arts Institute of
Design Archaeology Projet
II, 1936.

gained an appreciation of enduring design values through the reconstruction of histori-cal paradigms representative of various building cultures. At first glance, student drawings from the Montana years appear to belong to an entirely different design milieu. In 1951, for example, William Laffan (class of 1952) won a prize for his design for a "Building for a Glass Distributor." In terms of the design problem (a contemporary commercial building rather than an archaeological monument), the primary material (glass rather than stone), and design values (transparent volumes rather than solid masses), Laffan's drawing testifies to the emergence of a modernist design sensibility within the Department of Architecture.

If we accept this "snapshot" view of the past at face value, the implications seem clear: A conception of design education based on the careful study of past accomplish-ments and techniques is jettisoned for a design program based on modern materials, structural techniques and an absolute rejection of historical precedent. This line of argument supports an interpretation of American architecture at midcentury that describes a dramatic change in design and design education prompted by the arrival of a generation of European emigré architects like Ludwig Mies van der Rohe, Walter Gropius, and Marcel Breuer, who assume influential positions within the educational and professional practice establishments. On the microscale of one department, the Notre Dame experience repeats a phenomenon apparent on the macroscale of America as a whole: Change is revolutionary rather than evolutionary; traditionalists are "defeated" by an insurgent modernist movement composed of men disdainful of the history. If, however, one refocuses the study of architectural history from the formal analysis of isolated designs identified as paradigmatic to a broader consideration of patterns and issues in design discourse over time, it is possible to challenge the accuracy of our historical "snapshot" and reconstruct a more subtle account of the past.

Our understanding of the Department of Architecture at midcentury must begin with a discussion of the Kervick years. Francis Kervick studied architecture at the University of Pennsylvania prior to joining the Notre Dame faculty in 1909. In his memoir, *My Notre Dame: Memories and Reflections of Sixty Years,* Thomas Stritch included this portrait of Kervick:

> He was charmingly old-fashioned . . . his favorite painter was Frank Brangwyn. That was the kind of visual art he loved, simple, sweet, formal, good, but utterly conventional. . . . Kervick seemed a quiet mousey person, but under his reserved exterior he was thoroughly opinionated. He hated modern architecture and shrugged off the plans Frank Lloyd Wright drew up for Notre Dame's expansion in 1923. He adored the Gothic style. He was, of course, in the swim: Yale, Princeton and West Point led the 1920s in an outpouring of collegiate Gothic building in the United States.[1]

Figure 40.
Francis Kervick

Kervick translated his love of Gothic into a series of notable designs for the Notre Dame campus, including Memorial Porch to the east transept of the Basilica of the Sacred Heart, and, along with his associate, Vincent Fagan (class of 1920), Kervick is responsible for Howard, Morrissey and Lyons residence halls and Cushing Hall, home for the College of Engineering. He also played an instrumental role in securing the South Dining Hall commission for Ralph Adams Cram, who was, at the time, the leading advocate of Gothic design in America, and Kervick and Fagan were the associated architects for this project.

Much of Kervick's scholarly research was devoted to recovering and documenting the history of Catholic architects active in America, and he published two books on the subject.[2] His own practice included designs for Catholic churches in this country and abroad. Appropriately, given Kervick's lifelong involvement with church architecture, it is in the pages of the souvenir book, published in 1935, for the dedication of a small parish church in East Chicago, Indiana, that he expressed his own view of the role of the architect and the nature of the design process.

Figure 41.
Kervick & Fagan Architects, Lyons Hall, east elevation. 1925.

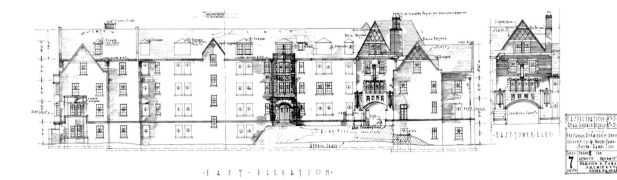

·EAST·ELEVATION·

When an architect is asked to design a building, he must work intelligently, know something of the people who are to occupy the structure. He must know their characteristics, their tastes and traditions and also the amount of money that is available in order to give them the sort of building that they anticipate. Disregarding these factors produces too often a building such as the architect himself fancies or tries to make a monument to himself.[3]

Significantly, Kervick did not let his personal commitment to Gothic design and his antipathy for modern architecture blind him to his obligations as an educator. His own education and subsequent travels abroad convinced Kervick of the value inherent in academic training based on the French model of the École des Beaux-Arts and, in the late 1920s, Notre Dame became associated with a national educational program based on the École model: the Beaux-Arts Institute of Design, headquartered in New York City. No account of architectural education at Notre Dame during the middle decades of this century is complete without a discussion of this national educational association.

The story of the Beaux-Arts Institute of Design begins in 1894 with the founding of the Society of Beaux-Arts Architects in New York City.[4] The membership of this society consisted of American architects trained at the École des Beaux-Arts in Paris who desired, in their words: "to cultivate and perpetuate the principles and associations of the École des Beaux-Arts."[5] Among its other activities, the Society of Beaux-Arts Architects quickly developed an educational program for young draftsmen in New York offices designed to inculcate the principles of the French academic training among American students unable to attend the Parisian École. The success of this educational program soon recommended it to architectural programs outside New York, and

Figure 42.
William Laffan. Building for a Glass Distributor. Kawneer Prize, Beaux-Arts Institute of Design, 1951.

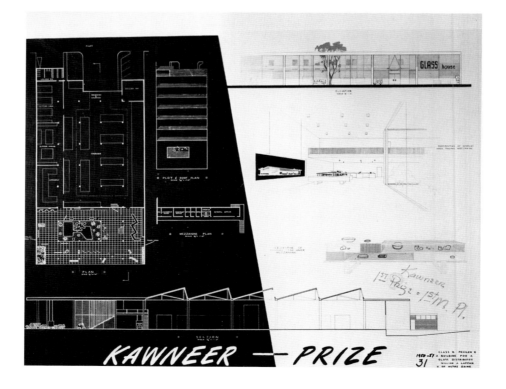

the demand for some type of national program led to the creation of a nonprofit educational institute known as the Beaux-Arts Institute of Design (hereafter: the BAID) chartered by the New York State Board of Regents in 1916.[6] The BAID periodically distributed design problems to participating institutions, collected student work submitted by member schools, arranged for design juries composed of practicing architects to evaluate the student work and published the results of jury deliberations in its *Bulletin of the Beaux-Arts Institute of Design*. At its peak, in the early 1930s, thousands of students participated in design problems ranging from nine-hour sketch problems to five-week studio problems. During the academic year 1929–30, 2,466 students from 44 different American educational programs submitted 9,622 drawings to be juried at the New York offices of the BAID.[7] Reduced enrollments in colleges and universities brought about by the Great Depression of the 1930s, and later by the Second World War affected the number of submissions to BAID programs in the late 1930s and '40s, but it continued to play an active national role in American architectural education well into the postwar era.

The *Bulletin of the BAID* scrupulously published detailed reports of jury discussions. The number of students submitting designs for each problem were noted, jury deliberations were summarized, and award-winning designs were illustrated. The BAID believed that publishing the results of its deliberations served several important roles.

This work provides a basis, on a national scale, for the comparative judging of student work. The fact that programs and critical reports are written by, and problems judged by, prominent practicing architects creates an important link between the academic world and the practicing profession.[8] Reading past issues of the *Bulletin* today allows us to eavesdrop on conversations held decades ago and recover something of the spirit and enthusiasm characteristic of an earlier era.

Both of the projects mentioned earlier — Beltemacchi's "Etruscan Gate" and Laffan's "Building for a Glass Distributor" — were submitted originally as solutions to problems assigned by the BAID, and jury deliberations for each were dutifully reported in the *Bulletin*.[9] The same 1936 issue that reported the outcome of the Etruscan gate archaeological problem also presented the results of an architectural problem involving the design of a canning factory assigned by the BAID. Unfortunately, none of the illustrated submissions were by Notre Dame students, although several had submitted drawings. All of the premiated and illustrated designs were unequivocally modern in character, featuring asymmetrical compositions of flat-roofed, extensively glazed volumes with little, if any, applied ornament and no historical references. In retrospect, what is striking about the canning-factory problem is the evident affinity between the solutions proposed in 1936 and the approach adopted by William Laffan in his 1951 design for a glass distribution facility. Already in 1936, the modernist credo of "Form Follows Function" is being explored in American schools of architecture — including Notre Dame as is evident in other issues of the *Bulletin* from these years. A review of student work submitted to the BAID over the course of several decades beginning in the late 1920s fails to support accounts of American architecture predicated on the notion of a sudden, revolutionary reorientation of design in the years after World War II. Instead, it appears that modern and traditional architectural ideals coexisted in American architectural culture of the late 1920s and '30s and that in studios at the University of Notre Dame, as elsewhere, a vigorous debate about the relative merits of each thrived. The BAID constituted an important point of intersection for the worlds of professional practice and architectural education and thus did much to nurture this lively debate.[10]

Figure 43.

Frank Montana during his Paris Prize
year, 1936.

Frank Montana, who eventually succeeded Kervick as chairman of the
Department of Architecture at Notre Dame, first gained national recogni-
tion as a result of his participation in the BAID. Montana graduated from
New York University in 1933 and in 1936 received the BAID's prestigious
Paris Prize. Awarded annually to recent architectural graduates, the Paris
Prize subsidized a year of postgraduate study at the École des Beaux-Arts in Paris.
Upon his return from Paris, the BAID staged a one-man show of Montana's drawings in
New York.[11] Thus, when he joined the Notre Dame faculty in 1939, Montana arrived
with a national reputation, a familiarity with the BAID system and firsthand knowledge
of the Paris École. Montana's account of his own experience at the École also indicated
that he was well aware of the international debates surrounding the École method of
teaching architecture.

> The social and technical conditions of our age, have started a new
> trend and while many who condemned the Beaux-Arts, saying it too
> traditional, meaning that it has classical tendencies and that it has not
> used novel fantastic forms, the fact is that the École has used and
> produced new ideas and will continue to teach a sane and lasting
> architecture based on the use of good logic and new materials; an
> architecture full of feeling and beauty obtained from the simplest
> forms. . . . The school is working against the abuse of modern
> architecture.[12]

Montana's own work in this period reveals his interest in the popular version of modern architecture often identified today by the labels Art Deco or Moderne. With Montana's arrival at Notre Dame, one begins to note an increasing diversity and sophistication in work submitted for consideration by the BAID and greater student success in BAID competitions. In 1945, for example, Notre Dame received the annual medal presented to the school that had earned the most awards in BAID-sponsored design problems the previous year.[13]

The academic structure of the architecture program was reconfigured several times during the Kervick and Montana years. When Kervick assumed the chairmanship in 1920, architecture was a department in the College of Engineering. It offered two four-year degrees in architecture: one designated as a design program, the other an architectural engineering sequence. In 1935–36, one five-year program replaced these two separate degree tracks. In 1941, the architectural degree program was reduced in length to four years, and a few years later, in 1944, the two-track curriculum leading to separate degrees in design or architectural engineering was reinstated. Finally, in 1948, the present five-year degree program was established.[14] If attempts at Notre Dame to define precisely the architectural degree demonstrate parallels with other American colleges and universities in these years, one significant development established the Notre Dame program as unique. In 1969, Montana instituted a Rome Study Center for the Department of Architecture. While many American architectural programs provide optional or supplemental study abroad opportunities for their students, only at Notre Dame is it a mandatory part of the curriculum for every architecture student.

Figure 44.
Frank Montana. Guérande, France, 14 August 1937.

The late 1940s and early '50s constitute a dynamic chapter in the history of the architecture program at Notre Dame. New courses in housing and city planning — reflecting the social agenda of modern architecture — were added to the curriculum, thus filling a curious gap in the BAID and Parisian École sets of studio exercises, which tended to ignore these important design issues. The influence of the venerable French École des Beaux-Arts began to wane as the Notre Dame faculty grew in number and acquired an increasingly international flavor. In 1945, Vito Girone began teaching architectural design at Notre Dame. Girone's background included experience with the BAID program during his student years at New York University and a year at the École des Beaux-Arts at Fontainebleau, France, in 1937. His résumé also listed stints at the New School for Social Research in New York and Cranbrook Academy in Bloomfield Hills, Michigan, both centers of progressive thinking about design and planning in the 1930s. Twin brothers Victor and Aladar Olgyay from Hungary joined the staff in 1948, and Victor taught a two-semester sequence entitled "Principles of City Planning." In 1949, Otto Seeler joined Notre Dame faculty and taught design and building technology. A product of the German technical university system rather than the French Beaux-Arts school, Seeler arrived at Notre Dame after teaching at Frankfurt and Darmstadt in Germany and Havana, Cuba. Two years later, Ernst Brandl, a protégé of the Viennese architect Adolf Loos, began teaching at Notre Dame. Austrian by birth, Brandl was educated in Vienna and during the early 1930s served as an architectural consultant for the municipal administration of that city. Forced to flee Hitler's Europe, he taught briefly in England before coming to the United States in 1947. From 1951 until his retirement in 1965, Brandl taught the history of architecture courses and played a

Figure 45.
Vito Girone   Figure 46.
Aladar Olgyay   Figure 47.
Victor Olgyay

Figure 48.
Otto Seeler   Figure 49.
Ernst Brandl

Figure 50.
Paul Grillo leads a class discussion in studio, c1956.

major role in the cultural and intellectual life of the school.[15] French architect Paul Grillo joined the faculty in 1952 and attempted to introduce a theory of organic design largely at odds with the Beaux-Arts conception of architecture. His acclaimed 1960 book *What is Design?* pulls together many of the ideas, insights and arguments that informed his teaching at Notre Dame.[16] Throughout the 1950s, Notre Dame students and faculty vigorously debated the relative merits of celebrated monuments of classical architecture, examples of anonymous vernacular design and buildings conceived in terms of new materials and technologies as models for contemporary architectural design.

   One of the themes of this essay has been the balance between traditional and modern conceptions of architecture within the Notre Dame program. The slow, patient search for a proper balance between the enduring virtues of the past and the emerging opportunities of the present was at the heart of architectural education not only at Notre Dame but also in schools across the United States during the period surveyed here. For institutions like the University of Notre Dame and professions like architecture, the pace of change is not as important as the care and rigor with which ideas are evaluated, opportunities are explored, and all sides of a debate are heard. Notre Dame's participation in the BAID served the University well; it provided an arena in which Notre Dame students could measure their work against their peers nationally. In the pages of the BAID's *Bulletin,* they could observe the leading practitioners and educators of their time discussing the broad outlines of an architecture respectful of the past and appropriate for the present.

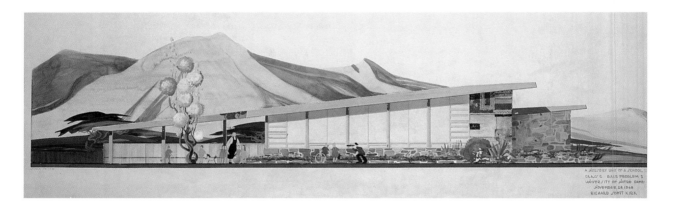

Figure 51.
Ventura Gonzalez.
A House in Texas. c1947.

Figure 52.
Richard Scott Kirk.
A Nursery Unit of a
School. Mention, Beaux-
Arts Institute of Design,
Class C, Problem II, 1949.

In 1949, the BAID issued a sketch problem for the design of a stained glass window. The program called for a window to be installed in a "frankly contemporary" church constructed of reinforced concrete. The jury deliberations, reported by Maurice Lavanoux,[17] editor of the influential journal *Liturgical Arts,* capture the ethos of American architectural culture — and architectural education at Notre Dame — at midcentury. Lavanoux wrote:

> It may be that students of art, nowadays, are prone to believe that a new "contemporary" freedom implies a freedom to jettison all tradition, whereas this new life . . . is but a logical continuation of tradition . . . we must not disregard the gold chain of tradition but we must seek to add our link and not be content with the futile job of repolishing the ancient links. What is to be sought for is a living tradition.[18]

For more than five decades, in various campus "homes" and curricular configurations, Francis Kervick, Frank Montana and their faculty ensured that the quest for a "living tradition" remained alive at the University of Notre Dame.

■ ■ ■

ENDNOTES

1. Thomas Stritch, *My Notre Dame: Memories and Reflections of Sixty Years* (Notre Dame: University of Notre Dame Press, 1991), 116, 238. No record of Wright's scheme for the Notre Dame campus survived. This episode is described by Thomas Schlereth in his campus history *The University of Notre Dame. A Portrait of its History and Campus* (Notre Dame: University of Notre Dame Press, 1991), 142–144.

2. Francis W. Kervick, *Architects in America of Catholic Tradition* (Rutland, Vt.: C.E.Tuttle Co., 1962) and *Patrick Charles Keely, Architect; A Record of His Life and Work* (South Bend, Ind.: Priv. print, 1953).

3. Francis W. Kervick, "The Architect Speaks" in *A Memento of the Dedication of the Church of the Immaculate Conception, East Chicago, Indiana* (15 September 1935), 11.

4. "The History and Aims of the Society of Beaux-Arts Architects," *The American Architect* 95 (1909): 101–102.

5. *Society of Beaux-Arts Architects Constitution* (New York: 1910), 1.

6. Otto Teegen, "The B.A.I.D. — its Past and Future," *Journal of the American Institute of Architects* 20 (October 1953): 182–189.

7. Ibid., 184.

8. Ibid., 183.

9. "Reports of Judgement: An Etruscan Gate," *The Bulletin of the Beaux-Arts Institute of Design* 12 (February 1936): 10–13; "A Building for a Glass Distributor," *The Bulletin of the Beaux-Arts Institute of Design* 27 (February 1951): 21–25.

10. See, for example, Seth Talcott, "The Modern Approach to Architecture," *The Bulletin of the Beaux-Arts Institute of Design* 15 (February 1939): 2–3; this is a report of a BAID-sponsored debate about contemporary architecture between the modernist Walter Dorwin Teague (then on the Board of Design for the 1939 New York World's Fair) and the traditionalist William G. Perry (prominently identified with the restoration of colonial Williamsburg).

11. "Exhibition by Frank Montana, 29th Paris Prize, 1936, and His Account of the École des Beaux-Arts in Paris," *The Bulletin of the Beaux-Arts Institute of Design* 15 (October 1939): 2–4.

12. Ibid., 3.

13. "Notre Dame Department of Architecture Awarded a Medal," *The Scholastic* 83 (19 January 1945): 6.

14. For a detailed account of the various degree program configurations see: Philip Moore, C.S.C. *Academic Development: Past, Present and Future* (University of Notre Dame: 1960), 79–84.

15. This influx of new faculty into the Architecture program echoed developments in other departments and reflected the growth of the University as a whole in the late 1940s and early 1950s. During Father John Cavanaugh's tenure as president of Notre Dame (1946–52), overall student enrollment grew by 62 percent and dozens of European scholars joined the University's faculty.

16. Michael D. Feord, "People Behind Notre Dame: A Profile of Ernst Brandl," *The Scholastic* 116 (25 April 1975): 19.

17. Paul Grillo, *What is Design?* (Chicago: Paul Theobald, 1960).

18. Lavanoux was a prominent figure in the Liturgical Arts Society and an expert of issues pertaining to Catholic liturgical design. His participation as a juror for BAID programs dealing with liturgical design is an indication of the seriousness with which liturgical design issues were treated by the BAID. For more on the Liturgical Arts Society see: Susan White, *The Liturgical Arts Society (1927–1972): Art and Architecture in the Agenda of the American Roman Catholic Liturgical Renewal* (Ph.D. Dissertation, University of Notre Dame: 1987).

19. Maurice Lavanoux, "A Stained Glass Window: Report of the Jury," *The Bulletin of the Beaux-Arts Institute of Design* 25 (May 1949): 60–61.

Up 100 Steps for Architecture:

A Student Memoir from 1928

■ ■ ■

C. ARNOLD THOMA

What was it like to be in the Architectural School during the 1924–28 period? The first thing that comes to mind was the climb of around 100 steps, at least once a day to the top floor of the Main Building where the department was located. And when our projects were in the finishing stages and every moment counted we would make four or five trips a day, sometimes for a week or more. Figuring roughly an average of two trips a day, 216,000 steps in four years, and that would be the minimum. Perhaps that is the reason it's so tough climbing stairs these days.

Our projects took so much time in those days because all architectural drawings were presented on stretched paper, inked and shades and shadows were dealt with meticulously. Every afternoon was spent in the Department with classes working on our projects, generally up to five o'clock.

The last few days before a project was due was cram time and we would work as long as was necessary. I remember one pitch black night, in my senior year, at 4:30 a.m. heading for my room off campus on Notre Dame Avenue. Sometimes Day Dogs would sleep on the drafting tables rather than take the time to go home.

Our freshman year was fairly routine, probably due to our having one of the architectural seniors as an instructor. He was well liked and I guess we "cooled it" so that we wouldn't get him in trouble. But during our sophomore year, as our projects became larger in scope, the inevitable happened. It could have been a hop-skip-and-jump contest, a wrestling match, or whatever that made too much noise for the nth time, with the Carroll Hall dorm just below us. Anyway, the result was that after that the department was locked up every night at 10 o'clock.

At first we encountered this inconvenience by turning out the lights and hiding outside the dormer windows in the built-in gutter which was reasonably wide and safe enough. After observing the night watchman's routine several nights we found safer areas in the department to hide. By our junior year they were locking up on Saturdays, Sundays and holidays. This presented a real problem for the first to arrive. It meant climbing the fire escape, walking the gutter and entering through the dormer window. No one bothered us after we had maneuvered our way in, however, and it did accomplish their main purpose, to keep the area relatively quiet.

Figure 53. **C. Arnold Thoma, Class of 1928**

to keep them well hidden.

However, as soon as we started up the stairs we found we were in trouble for the bottles began to slip. I don't remember who first experienced the slipping but of course it was hilariously funny to the other. Luckily we were laughing at our predicament for the contortions we went through to save the bottles from exposure must have been attributed to our laughter. Anyway we made it to the top and a successful party but those 100 steps seemed like 300 that day. I'm sure some of our other parties had their problems but that was one I'll never forget.

On these late night sessions naturally we could not have survived without a midnight snack, and we took turns providing the food. On one occasion, when it was my turn, I found myself downtown for dinner and too late to get back to O.A. Clark's Cafeteria in Badin Hall, for the food. There was a deli just north of the Palais Royale dance hall, but it was Sunday and they were about cleaned out. However, they did have some apple turnovers in the window. Well, the snack lasted just one bite as the turnovers were moldy on the inside and wound up on the walls and ceiling. The next day we were given the ultimatum to clean up or else. Needless to say I bore the brunt of that episode.

One Saturday afternoon when we were winding up an especially long project we decided to celebrate the occasion. I and another loser, having drawn the short straws, set out for Nick's place to get four bottles of wine. For any who have forgotten, Nick's was a red brick house about a mile north of the campus on Eddy Road. (How could you forget Nick's? It was a great place to celebrate birthdays or any other good excuse.)

As we went down the stairs from the department all was quiet and serene. Nary a Reverend was in sight. Returning to the campus we found the serenity had disappeared and the Reverend Fathers were coming and going in all directions including up and down the stairs we had to climb. It must have been time for the afternoon walk. We still felt reasonably secure with two bottles each, tucked in our pants behind our belts with the sheepskin coats

Usually during the February doldrums, the upperclassmen would declare that the freshmen, having worked so hard up to then, had earned the right to join the "Royal Order of Sleepless Nights." The department library contained quite a few antique French helmets, spears, coats-of-mail and other armor which would be donned by the upperclassmen as perfect attire to give the event some "École des Beaux Arts" pizzazz. The freshmen were lined up and authoritatively marched, single file, to a 30 by 60-inch sink, filled with water, then dunked in turn, and properly knighted ceremoniously with a sword.

There were several bridge players in our class and regularly after the profs departed for the day we would play a few hands, as sort of a recess. There were times when we were ready to play, but weren't sure the profs had departed, so we would go out the dormer window, walk the gutter a few feet to a tin deck roof, about eight feet square, to enjoy our game. The view was great but usually it was quite a problem grabbing the cards before they blew off the roof.

Reprinted from *Before the Colors Fade: Some Memories by Members of the Class of 1928, University of Notre Dame: May 1983 for the 55th year reunion.* Special Collections, University Libraries.

Figure 54.
Class of 2000 students Aimée Catrow and Erin Christensen in the Bond Hall fourth-year studio.

A Glance Back

...

ROBERT L. AMICO

Prelude: Prepared and Eager

As an alumnus of Harvard University and the University of Illinois at Urbana-Champaign, but a "Domer" at heart, I am delighted to provide a glimpse of a portion of Architecture's 100-year history at the University of Notre Dame, particularly from the perspective of design education.

In 1978 I was appointed chairman and professor of architecture by Rev. Theodore M. Hesburgh, C.S.C. I arrived here from the University of Illinois at Urbana-Champaign, a highly regarded public research university, and an early leader in higher education in architecture in the United States.[1] Illinois offered one of the most comprehensive and largest professional degree programs and is a nationally recognized school with a broad approach to architecture and design education. There I taught all levels of design studio, advised 121 thesis students, and was honored by the Gargoyle Society for my academic contributions. I was elected chairman of architectural design (as large as the entire school at Notre Dame with 250 students), appointed member of the Graduate College, and advanced through the ranks to earn a full professorship at age 38.

I was well prepared for the chairmanship, with a solid but general knowledge of what was needed to continue to improve the architecture program. At Notre Dame, which, in contrast to Illinois, is a small, private, and, most importantly, Catholic university, I quickly discovered that I had a lot to learn, and did, with the patience and counsel of those with whom I came in contact.

Pedagogy: Academic Freedom and Balance

Trained in Beaux-Arts and Modern design curricula in architecture and urban design, and also as a tradesman carpenter during my university years, I apply a variety of approaches to design and architecture in higher education. The bottom line is: breadth and quality in professional degree programs. Ignore academic freedom, and become a trade school. Choose self-generated publicity over unbiased third-party open assessment, and you are a false institution — a mere facade. This fundamental concern for breadth and quality is part of the tradition of academic freedom, which warns against "dominant ways of thinking"[2] and "private institutes."[3]

My beliefs about education are very much in line with the principles expressed in the *Carnegie Report:*

> If anything is clear . . . there is no single "right" approach to architecture education, nor any single form of scholarship that ought to predominate. The need for diversity in programs and faculty talent is, in fact, more urgent than ever as a changing job climate has made it essential that graduates leave school prepared to move among careers within, and beyond, "traditional" practice.[4]

The *Report* further states:

> In the context of higher education, the learning community rejects prejudicial or dogmatic judgments, honors diversity, and seeks to serve effectively and empower the full range of people in society.[5]

To offer students less would be an insult to them, discriminating against the amount and type of knowledge they receive, and seriously shortchanging them in terms of learning and financial investment. Fortunately, the School of Architecture is deeply rooted in the strong balance between traditional and modern notions of architecture and design — from previous chairmen Francis Kervick, Frank Montana and Ambrose Richardson to my own chairmanship.

Foundation Stones: Chairman 1978–89

In my very first, and last, comprehensive wish-list letter to Provost Tim O'Meara at the outset of my chairmanship, I enumerated what Architecture needed to continue its building process: additional faculty and staff; independent "school" status; an endowed graduate degree program in architecture (with graduate faculty, research and teaching assistantships, and facility); a larger budget; individual computers for the staff and faculty; an in-house computer facility for students; an associate/assistant chairperson; a chaired professorship; a full-time trained architectural historian; additional student awards; permanent program status and facilities for the Rome course of studies and a Chicago architecture center to formalize the Rome-Chicago connection. I also sought to build on the contributions of my predecessors, Frank Montana, founder of the junior year course of studies in Rome for the professional degree program, and Ambrose Richardson, unprecedented two-term president of the National Architectural Accrediting Board (NAAB), as well as an experienced practitioner and excellent teacher.

As continuing members of the faculty, I had the benefit of the wisdom, support and friendship Frank and Ambrose were willing to share with me, and I set out to strengthen and improve what existed: a somewhat balanced professional degree program in architecture in need of tuning, additional rigor, and organization; a dedicated, diverse, balanced (traditional and modern) yet independent-minded faculty; a bright, varied, and a-delight-to-work-with student body, and a good, but inadequate architecture building. I used this wish list during my chairmanship to reinforce our needs and to measure our progress. Our challenge was to improve, and we did! Our achievements are summarized in *Architecture at Notre Dame, Report of the Chairman 1978–89;* while examples of student work from that time, showing a range of approaches, appear in the *Notre Dame Architecture Review* of spring 1982.

Three major goals were accomplished with an emphasis on architecture and urbanism and the "Rome-Chicago Connection" for undergraduate professional degree and graduate post-professional degree students alike. These were: 1) an endowed post-professional graduate degree program in architecture in 1985 (initially funded with substantial resources to establish the Bond-Montedonico Fellowship Program, and the Joseph Z. Burgee and the Joseph Z. Burgee Jr. Fellowship program); 2) the permanent Rome Architecture Center with the University's purchase of a portion of a 400-year-old palazzo and its complete refurbishment in 1986; and 3) the development of the Chicago Architecture Center in 1988.

In 1986, the name for the junior-year curriculum in the professional degree program "Rome Course of Studies" was changed to the "Rome Architecture Center" to reflect the establishment of the post-professional degree program in architecture, and the expansion of the school's mandatory programs abroad. An NAAB accredited professional degree option in the graduate program was begun in 1994.

Frank Montana was critical to the permanent establishment of our presence in Rome. In short, when I arrived at Notre Dame, Otto Seeler was Rome director, and Frank Montana had retired. When Otto retired in 1979–80, I coaxed Frank out of retirement and appointed him Rome director again. The rest is history. We were successful and at last had a permanent new home away from home for our students in the heart of the Eternal City.

Toward the end of my tenure as chairman, I recall pumping a great deal of energy into the Chicago Architecture Center, the last of the three links in my portion of the chain. Funding was arranged; support from the City of Chicago and its planning department was secured; endorsement by the American Institute of Architects Chicago Chapter was received; and pursuit of studio and housing was under way.

The "Rome-Chicago Connection" would have been the first of its kind and would have preceded Columbia University's unique "The Shape of Two Cities: New York-Paris" program. Although this project was postponed, Chicago has been used as a design laboratory in various studios over the past 10 years, and the center has now been brought back to high priority by our new chairman William Westfall.

Full-term NAAB accreditation was received in 1989, and with that achievement I completed my service as chairman. Most of the wish-list items had been realized (or set down to be achieved at a later time), and the foundation had been laid for a solid future. Even preliminary conversations with alumnus William Bond, principal benefactor of the graduate program, were under way regarding the renovation of the Architecture Building.

Figure 55.
Robert L. Amico

In the Design Studio: Professor 1990–Present

That architecture . . . by nature and tradition, holds vast potential as a model for the integration and application of learning, largely because of its most distinctive feature — *the design studio.* For most of this century, design has dominated the architecture curriculum at nearly all schools. It is a *place* — the design studio — where students spend as much as 90 percent of their time and energy.[6]

My expertise lies in the design studio, termed the "distinctive holy-of-holies of architecture education."[7] It has concentrated on fifth-year design, in the thesis studio, where I have advised over 100 students, and in courses that surround and support this culminating effort: "Special Projects in Advanced Design," "Advanced Design and Thesis Preparation," and a course no longer offered, "Design Thesis Development," which the 1994 NAAB accreditation report praised as one in which ". . . students [have] the opportunity to investigate the details of their design in a wonderfully unique way."[8] After leaving my administrative duties, I found returning to the design studio refreshed my professional commitment and renewed my excitement about working with students again.

As a design studio professor, my goals are best expressed by the many beautiful words I have received from my students over the years. The following is but one example: "He is our friend and our mentor, and he wants what's best for all of us. He wants to see everyone be successful."

My approach is represented by design studio examples from classical to avant-garde, five projects that have been recognized at the school, regional, national and international levels. (See Figures 57 to 67.) These projects were firsts for the school and collectively embody precisely the view of higher education put forth by President Edward A. Malloy, C.S.C., in his 1992 Sesquicentennial Declaration following the celebration of Mass: "Notre Dame's first commitment is to freedom of inquiry and expression. Belief . . . should widen, not narrow our purview, and a Catholic university should be especially open to all truth and human insight."

Figure 56.

The Kinetic Skyscraper® team: Kathryn Schuth, Bob Amico, Paul Down, David Cutler, Michael Sullivan (standing), Sheila Delaney and Bryan Fox, 1999.

Figures 57 and 58.
Research, and Special Project in Advanced Design, 1986.

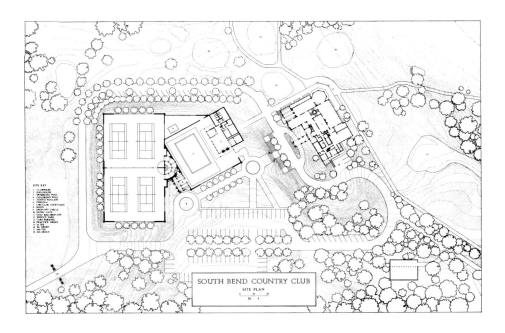

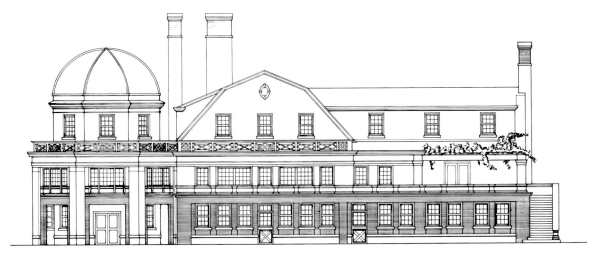

SOUTHEAST

"A Classical Alteration and Addition, Country Club House and Estate, South Bend, Indiana" by Luis Baldo, Daniel Keating, Alfredo Marr and Mary O'Toole.
Winner of the Chicago Award; sponsored by the Chicago Chapter of the American Institute of Architects; exhibited in the Art Institute of Chicago; published in the AIA Chicago awards catalog, and reported by WNDU Television. (The only classical/traditional design at Notre Dame to win this prestigious award.)
The project was aided in part by a grant of $4,000 from the South Bend Country Club.

Figures 59 (left), 60 (above) and 61 (below).
Design Thesis, 1995; and Design Thesis Development, 1996.

"Architecture as Product: The Hard Dive Café, Chicago, Illinois" by Marco Diez. Exterior Perspective, Interior and Elevator Cab.
Invited participant and representative from the University of Notre Dame; Certificate of Merit, one of 10 student awards in the
Midwest District Conference of the Industrial Designers Society of America; sponsored by the Industrial Designers Society of
America in Kansas City, Missouri. Team taught with associate professor of art and design, industrial designer Paul Down.

Figures 62 and 63.
Research, and Special Project in Advanced Design, 1998–

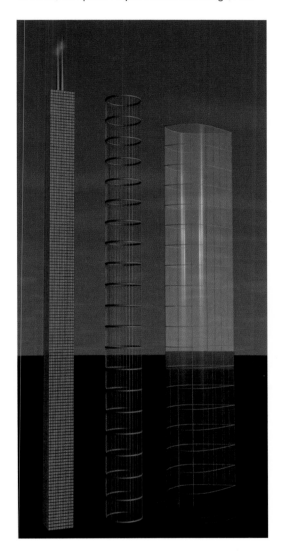 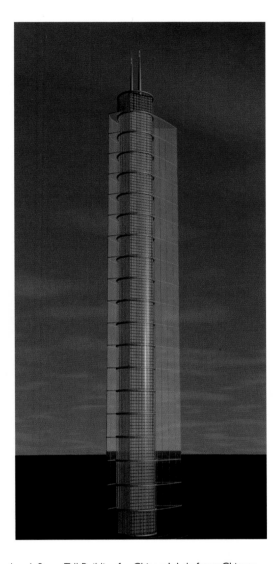

"The Kinetic Skyscraper®: A Proposal for the Smart Design of a Landmark Super Tall Building for Chicago's Lakefront; Chicago, Illinois" by Shelley Hoenle, Geoffrey Locksmith, Christopher Podstawski and Jennifer Rice.
Invited participants, World Conference on Structural Control, Kyoto, Japan (professional competition held once every four years); sponsored by the International Association for Structural Control; published by Wiley and Sons of Sussex, England. Codirector with former assistant professor, engineer I-Kwang Chang. The project was aided by a grant from the National Science Foundation. 1998–Present.
"It isn't often that an undergraduate project is given such significant international attention as is the case with the kinetic skyscraper," said Hoenle. "Being recognized on an international level is an honor to our school and the University. The project brings a breadth of scope to the architecture school," said Locksmith. "This proves that we are capable of other things, as well as designing traditional architecture."
The Observer (February 25, 1998), 1.
Work on this project is being continued by the team of David Cutler, Sheila Delaney, Kathryn Schuth, Michael Sullivan and Bryan Fox with associate professor of art and design, industrial designer Paul Down as consultant.

Figures 64 and 65.
Design Thesis, 1992.

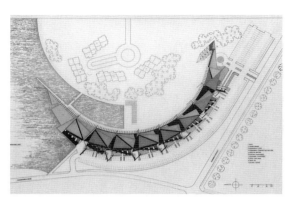 

"A Dynamic Architecture: Office and Retail Center, Ganada, New York" by Timothy Slattery.
First Prize, EnCharrette Exhibition sponsored by the Chicago Atheneum and Chicago Chapter of the American Institute of Architects; and winner of the Sollitt Award for Best Design Thesis in the School of Architecture.

Figures 66 and 67.
Special Project in Advanced Design, 1997.

 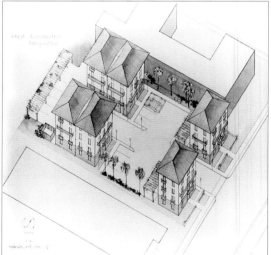

"Rehousing Hollywood: A Traditional Approach Using Contemporary Technology; Low Rise High Density Infill Housing for Low/ Moderate Income Families in High Seismic Sensitive Areas" by Jan Noethe, Aimee Propes, Christiane Fashek and Malika Kim. First Prize, National Competition ($1,000) sponsored by the Federal Emergency Management Agency, and American Institute of Architects Research; published by the Association of Collegiate Schools of Architecture in *Rehousing Hollywood, Results of the 1997 Student Design Competition.* Team taught with former assistant professor, engineer I-Kwang Chang; the codirectors received national fellowships to the Faculty Institute on Teaching Seismic Design in San Francisco.

Postscript: New Foundations

I have sought to make my fundamental concern for breadth and quality characteristic of my chairmanship and, subsequently, my teaching. The students have always been at the heart of my efforts in both instances. They are my greatest reward, and my gratitude to them has manifested itself in my establishment of the Amico Architecture Scholarship in 1997, awarded annually to a fifth-year student in the professional degree program, albeit a modest award at this time. The first recipient, in 1998, was Anthony Goldsby. This prize follows the establishment of the Chairman's Award for Design Excellence for the Fifth Year Thesis, which I initiated during my chairmanship in 1982, the same year the department was named a "school," and began the process of becoming autonomous from the College of Engineering. The establishment of the Amico and Chairman's awards follows the tradition set by former chairmen Francis Kervick, with the Kervick awards founded in honor of his mother and father, and Frank Montana, with the establishment of the Rome Scholarship.

My time at Notre Dame has passed ever so quickly. It is difficult for me to believe that I have been a part of the School of Architecture for two of its 10 decades of history. During this period, the students have brought great joy and satisfaction to my life. God willing, I hope that I can continue my work with them for another decade to come as together we lay the foundations for their careers in architecture and life.

■ ■ ■

ENDNOTES

1. The Massachusetts Institute of Technology was founded in 1867 and the architecture program at Illinois two years later in 1869.
2. Gerhard Casper, ninth president of Stanford University, "Inaugural Address," 2 October 1992.
3. Peter Rowe, "Dean's Day Address," Harvard University Graduate School of Design, 24 October 1992.
4. Ernest L. Boyer and Lee D. Mitgang, *Building Community: A New Future for Architecture Education and Practice: A Special Report* (Princeton, N.J.: Carnegie Foundation for the Advancement of Teaching, 1996), 52.
5. Ibid., 91.
6. Ibid., 85.
7. Ibid., xvii.
8. National Architectural Accreditation Board. Visiting Team Report: 12–16 February 1994, Part VII: team comments, 20.

Figure 68.
Marie Andree Soundy. Sant'Agnese,
Piazza Navona, Roma. 1995.

Reconnecting With Classicism

...

THOMAS GORDON SMITH

The teaching of architecture at Notre Dame for 100 years is a remarkable achievement. The examination of this period of time demonstrates the variety of administrative roles the discipline has played in the University. It also reflects the larger movements in architectural culture through changes in the curriculum and selection of faculty.

The last decade of the centenary has witnessed an especially dramatic shift and forceful development of profile. This has been achieved through the establishment of the School of Architecture at Notre Dame as the recognized leader in teaching the classical system of architecture and traditional urbanism. This change has brought challenges to commonly held assumptions of architectural theory that still dominate most schools and many of the published offices.

Students from Notre Dame are praised and sought after by a growing number of astute practitioners. It is said that they are uniquely qualified to enter traditional architectural and urbanist planning offices and "hit the ground running." In addition, the distinguished architect and educator Jacquelin Robertson (Cooper, Robertson & Partners) mentioned recently that the alumni show every indication of making significant independent contributions two decades hence. We will have to wait for the celebration of 125 years to assess their impact.

In the spring of 1989 I was interviewed for the chairmanship and presented a plan to bring classicism to the School of Architecture at Notre Dame. Thanks to the support of Stanley Tigerman, I had taught classical architecture at the University of Illinois at Chicago for three years. This was a wonderful opportunity, but the subject matter was basically inserted as an antidote to the dominant deconstruction and normative modernism taught at Chicago. Although I appreciated Tigerman's support, I began to yearn for a situation in which the classical language and theoretical point of view could be taught as a long and fully integrated program of study instead of as a semester-long, one-time event.

Quite by providence, I became aware of the search for the chairman at Notre Dame. Two aspects of the existing program struck me as indicators of potential receptivity to developing a thorough classical curriculum. First, several faculty members were pushing the Cornell concepts of Colin Rowe forward and Rowe himself was teaching in Rome. Second, the full year of study in Rome with its "compulsory" attendance had been in place for almost two decades and had clear signs of support from the University.

In interviewing for the job, I sensed administrative curiosity and interest in the proposal to reformulate the curriculum following traditional paradigms. This was partially due to Notre Dame's continuing respect for the humanistic tradition. It also seemed sparked by the inherent radicalism of the proposal. In retrospect, I am convinced that Notre Dame's administration is the only one in the United States that would have supported the classical proposal for the School of Architecture. In addition, it has shown deep and continual generosity toward the school during the subsequent decade and this has been far greater than anyone could have foreseen in 1989.

I was fortunate to be the successful candidate for the chairmanship and began work in the summer of 1989. It was possible to make several faculty appointments immediately and others over the following years. Gradually, this made the concept of a classical school more and more real. Without the support that allowed building the faculty with people well trained and committed to the cause, I could not have achieved much. The new faculty also found support from some older members, and even when conceptual issues were poles apart, collegiality and goodwill overcame divisions.

In fall 1989, I began to teach a second-year design course based on learning the proportions of Doric architecture and applying those elements to solve architectural and archaeological problems. By the end of the year, students redesigned the School of Architecture building, a real goal that with the help of the vice president for University Relations we were raising funds to achieve. This second-year syllabus set a new tone not only in terms of approach and subject matter but also in expectations. Although my proposed curriculum had been toned down by a wise former student, the 1989 second-year students were informed by the upper classes that they were working two or three times harder than before. No matter what the precise ratio, this course marked the beginning of ratcheting-up expectations of what students could accomplish throughout the School of Architecture curriculum. Despite the pain (normal to good architecture programs), the personal and professional gains are by now obvious.

Such radical changes in content and expectations prompted reaction, of course. My favorite was an article in *The Observer* that complained that my approach constrained personal expression and had turned the school into "a rigorous academy-like setting." This reputation for a distinct orientation and hard work is generally cited by undergraduate and graduate applicants as features that attract them to Notre Dame.

It is the faculty working with increasingly avid students who have really made the School of Architecture into a rigorous academy-like setting. Elsewhere, one can find the record of faculty publications and accomplishments in building and in the polemical world of debate on architectural issues. With a little more research one can also see the impact of the students and alumni, both in prominent offices and in competitions, exhibitions, publications and the growing establishment of organizations that promote the re-emergence of classical architecture and urbanism.

In addition to curricular development, the School of Architecture has grown with administrative and physical changes. From 1989 through 1991, the curriculum of the Rome Studies Program was changed so that the remarkable opportunity to study in this great paradigmatic city could be seamlessly integrated with the full classical curriculum.

The graduate program was expanded to offer an accredited degree. It has also expanded in size, partially due to the growth of its endowment. The growth of monetary opportunity has been paralleled by the applications of graduate students from remarkably diverse backgrounds who are deeply committed to the cause of classicism.

Thanks to support from the dean of the College of Engineering, Anthony N. Michel, the school emerged from its position as essentially a department within the college to achieve autonomous status directly under the Office of the Provost. Central to this administrative change were the efforts of the energetic School of Architecture Advisory Council. Finally, the former Lemonnier Library as a patched-together abode was given a long-awaited transformation to become Bond Hall. William and Joanne Bond, longtime supporters of the graduate endowment, contributed a major donation, which enabled the University to strip the building's interior down to the structure and reconfigure it. This created a functional and beautiful setting for teaching and research. An addition to the west created more square footage, improved circulation and a symbolic facade. Part of the new space was devoted to a rare book room to house new collections of historical editions of architectural books.

All the academic and structural changes of the past decade must be seen in the context of Notre Dame's aggressive desire to improve its effectiveness as an intellectual center. This drive has always been balanced by steadfast maintenance of the University's mission as a Catholic institution. Recent developments in the School of Architecture have contributed to that radical push to improve and expand. At the same time, we have reconnected with the most challenging sources of architectural and urbanistic tradition.

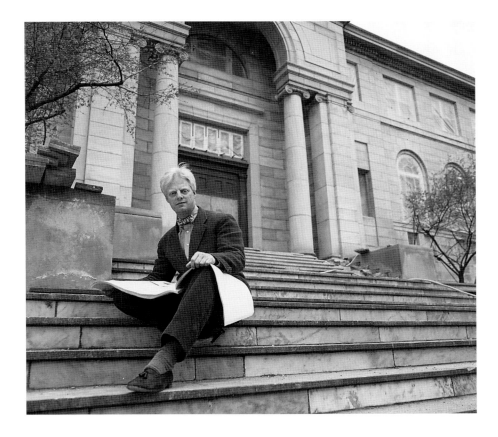

Figure 69.
Thomas Gordon Smith on the steps of the Architecture Building before its transformation into Bond Hall, 1995.

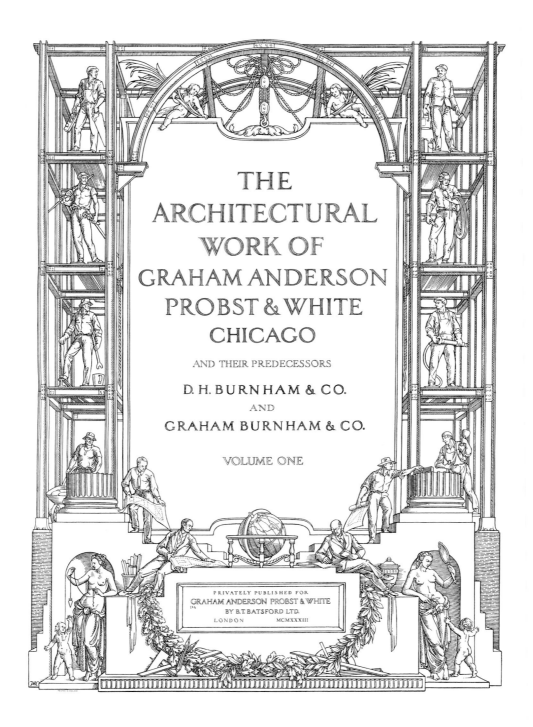

Figure 70.

James Canizaro. Title page for *The Architectural Work of Graham Anderson Probst & White, Chicago, and their Predecessors, D.H. Burnham Co. and Graham Burnham Co.*, 1933.

By the Book:

A History of the Architecture Library

■ ■ ■

JANE A. DEVINE

Throughout history, buildings have appeared and vanished, often without trace. Books offer a lasting record of what architects have designed and built, one that sometimes proves more enduring than architecture itself. Without them, the survival of architectural thought would be nearly impossible. As Adolf Placzek has observed: ". . . all past architecture is a concern of architectural literature, as is all future architecture — from the first huts to the cosmopolis of the 21st century."[1] Books and journals document not only what was built, but also unbuilt designs, utopian schemes and architects' ideas about their own work. The literature encompasses everything from theoretical treatises and critical studies to practical builders' guides and technical information. It is both textual and visual in nature, since it is difficult to discuss the creation of buildings without showing how they look. Published collections of drawings, sketches and architectural photographs thus form an important part of the historical record and a vital resource for the education of young architects.

The specialized architecture library was largely a 19th-century phenomenon, the result of new academic programs to educate architects and of the professional associations they formed.[2] The American Institute of Architects Library was established in 1857, the Avery Library at Columbia University in 1890, and the Art Institute of Chicago Burnham Library in 1912. Many professional firms also had their own libraries, which offered research material and a form of continuing education to their employees. In the private realm, clients, patrons, and untrained architects such as Thomas Jefferson often collected architectural books and shared their libraries with friends and colleagues.

The first glimpse of what would become the Notre Dame Architecture Library appears in the 1898–99 *Catalogue,* where the "Course in Architecture" makes its debut. Here it was stated:

> Those subjects that are not taught in the architect's office but which are necessary for an architect are especially insisted upon in this course. The work is technical and freehand drawing is thorough, and the student is prepared for the expression of his architectural plans. . . . The history of architecture is taught by lecture and illustrations. The material consists of plaster models, engravings and photographs of noted buildings, books on architecture, and the apparatus of the engineering and art schools.[3]

The fledgling program was housed on the top floor of the Administration Building, just above the library, which served the entire University. Early photographs suggest that some architecture books were gathered on shelves in the large drafting room where students spent a good part of their time. Other books were part of the main library's modest art and architecture collection.

By 1906, there was a clear need for more material to support the curriculum. The *Bulletin* noted that, although the newly designated College of Architecture had a collection of signed drawings, some by nationally known architects and others from the École des Beaux-Arts, as well as various models, photographs, reference books and manufacturers' catalogs, "the collection needs to be increased faster than the resources of the University will permit. Philanthropic friends of Notre Dame can not give money, or its equivalent, for a better purpose."[4] This request for donations heralded one strategy for collection building that continues to be important today.

Figure 71.

The Architects' Club in the Administration Building fifth-floor studio, 1912. The library is housed on the bookshelves behind them.

A s the program grew, so did the library. In 1923, the Department of Architecture could proudly assert that it possessed "an excellent collection of books on architecture, building construction, and the allied arts."[5] Chairman Francis Kervick doubtless played a significant role in expanding the library as he recruited new faculty and more students for the program. Records suggest that he was single-handedly in charge of the collection despite his teaching duties and work as a practicing architect. Books collected at the time reflected an interest in the French, British and Italian traditions central to the academic ideal of architecture in the early 20th century. Titles included works on Roman, Byzantine, classical and Gothic architecture and the palaces of Versailles and Fontainebleau. There were also books by landscape designer Gertrude Jekyll, Victorian Gothic architect Augustus Pugin and Edwin Lutyens, whose work exemplified both the British Arts and Crafts movement and a renewed form of classicism.[6]

The new University librarian, Paul Byrne, appointed in 1924, proved a good friend of the Architecture Library. It seems likely that his daily lunches with Kervick in the South Dining Hall resulted in greater support for the architecture collection, which received "special attention" and "special magazines" once Byrne took charge.[7] He also convinced the administration to double the annual library fee to $6 per student in 1929–30, which led to an increase in the annual funds for architecture from $170 to over $400.[8]

When the department moved into its own building in 1931, the library occupied a room on the first floor, where it contained "800 volumes devoted to construction and the history of architecture, the larger folios showing the historic masterpieces." Ten American and European architecture journals were also available to students and faculty.[9] This room in the Architecture Building (now Crowley Hall) was the first space devoted exclusively to the library, although there was as yet no staff to organize the collection or help users with research. Still, the move brought a much larger library budget that mirrored the growing status of the architecture program, its burgeoning enrollment and the library's increasing importance.

Despite Paul Byrne's dedication to developing the University libraries, he was not enthusiastic about departmental collections. In 1945, responding to pressure from faculty who wanted more literature available within their areas, he asserted:

> I have tried to make clear to the men in these various depart-
> ments that a departmental library is not expected to have at hand
> all of the books in their own particular field. [It] . . . is intended to
> be a working collection only. . . . By necessity there must be certain
> reference books easily available, a number of the more useful books
> in each subject and perhaps the current issues of certain of the
> periodicals. . . . Critics of modern education often point the finger
> of scorn at the present day college student because so many of them
> have been allowed to specialize in one subject to the exclusion of an
> interest in anything else. So the departmental library by segregating
> all of the important books in any given subject in a special collection
> does much in defeating the purpose of a well-rounded education.[10]

No doubt Byrne was also worried about spreading a very limited budget too thinly, particularly during the Depression and Second World War, when enrollment declined and recruiting library staff became very difficult. In the absence of a librarian, Francis

Figure 72.

Ida Bonicelli in the
Architecture Library, c1947.
To her right is a portrait
of Henry John Schlacks,
founder of the program.

Kervick and, from 1939, Frank Montana had been responsible for choosing library
books. Nonetheless, before long Byrne had to concede to faculty demand and acknowl-
edge the need to hire branch librarians. The National Architectural Accrediting Board
(NAAB) also required that accredited schools have libraries with professional staff, and
the department was preparing for the anticipated NAAB review in 1949. Ida Bonicelli
arrived with her twin sister, Irma, in the fall of 1946 and in early 1947 became the first
professional architecture librarian at Notre Dame, while Irma became the science
librarian. Ida's appointment coincided with a move from the first floor to the second
floor of the newly built Architecture Building annex. This new space included a reading
room and stack area with seating for 25 students and an adjacent librarian's office and
workroom.

    After nearly 50 years without a librarian, the collection was in lamentable condition,
and Ida Bonicelli set about organizing the library with admirable energy. She began
offering reference service and library instruction, started an index of architecture
journals not indexed elsewhere, prepared bibliographies to help students with Beaux-
Arts Institute of Design assignments and took over management of the slide collection.
By this time, the collection had grown to some 3,300 books, over 10,000 slides and
2,400 pamphlets.[11] Bonicelli provided all the services herself with the help of part-time
student assistants and, in the case of book selection, with the faculty's advice. She
brought far more than organizational and practical skills to her task. Her professional
background raised the library to a new level as an intellectual resource. Bonicelli's
broader perspective is shown in her report on architecture libraries, which describes

Notre Dame's program in relation to the NAAB requirements, the Association of Collegiate Schools of Architecture, the BAID program, and recent studies by Talbot Hamlin of Columbia University and historian Henry-Russell Hitchcock.[12]

Once management of the library was in the hands of a professional, the relationship with faculty remained close and collaborative. Professors recommended titles for purchase, and the librarian also made her own choices from reviews and publishers' catalogs. With the recruitment of European faculty members after the war such as Ernst Brandl, Otto Seeler, Paul Grillo, and Victor and Aladar Olgyay, the library began to reflect the Department of Architecture's growing diversity and the breadth of faculty research interests. Where previously primarily English-language journals were collected, by 1960 the library had added German, Japanese, Brazilian, Italian and Greek subscriptions.[13]

Notre Dame's main library had also grown to such an extent that a new building was needed. This provided the ideal opportunity for the Department of Architecture to leave its cramped quarters and move into the vacated Lemonnier Library, after the building was renovated according to Frank Montana's design in 1964. The new library facilities were on the north side of the building in the former reading room. They offered three times as much floor space and almost double the shelving and seating capacity of the previous location, along with glass display cases for exhibitions. Librarian Tobi Milonadis set up the new library and began working with Prof. Julian Kulski to expand the city planning collection, in anticipation of greater emphasis on urbanism in the curriculum.[14]

1964 also marked the arrival of Paul Sprague, the first architectural historian at Notre Dame. While the history of architecture had always been part of the program, it had usually been taught by well-traveled practicing architects such as Francis Kervick.

Figure 73.
The Architecture Library in its third location, c1970.

This tendency was typical of the approach in many schools, where students learned to recognize major monuments and to identify different periods and architectural styles but were not taught how to interpret and evaluate what they saw in a historical and theoretical framework. As Lawrence Anderson has observed, neither the Beaux-Arts tradition nor the Bauhaus emphasized architectural history or research within their standard curricula. The École favored work in the atelier over "bookish" study, while the Bauhaus-trained educators preferred students to learn design in the studio before exploring historical precedents.[15] American schools of architecture were influenced by these differing schools of thought, yet the unique legacy of American architectural education was its development into an academic discipline with a strong research foundation. As this occurred, the natural alliance between the librarian and the architectural historian became an influential force in developing library collections to support advanced research. Not only Sprague, but also those who succeeded him at Notre Dame, typically sat on the library advisory committee, advised on book selection and helped to assess ways to improve the collection.

During this period of ambitious growth at Notre Dame, two initiatives affected the library. In 1969 Frank Montana launched the Rome Studies Center, which had its own branch library run by local faculty. A year earlier, Prof. Patrick Horsbrugh had started the master's program in environic design, receiving a generous library budget to support the new courses. Librarian Geri Decker, who took over from Milonadis in 1965, worked with Horsbrugh to develop a collection in the interdisciplinary field of environmental design, which explored the ecological, social and economic impact of architecture and urban planning. Decker was also involved in urban renewal and historic preservation activities in the community and brought this commitment to her work. She was among the first members of the Association of Architectural Librarians founded at the 1975 American Institute of Architects convention and remained professionally active until her retirement in 1983.

Figure 74.
Librarian Geri Decker in her office, c1970.

The organizational status of the Architecture Library was, in some ways, anomalous. While the Department of Architecture had been part of the College of Engineering since 1920, its library had only briefly shared administration in the early 1940s, when a joint engineering libraries committee was formed to coordinate efforts between the main library and the chemical engineering, metallurgy and architecture libraries. Surprisingly, Architecture held more books than the Engineering Library itself at that time.[16] However, in 1985, the Architecture Library was brought under the wing of engineering librarian Robert Havlik, who assumed responsibility for the collection, aided by a branch supervisor who ran the daily operations. This practice continued until 1997, by which time the School of Architecture had become autonomous from the College of Engineering. A renewed need for professional management led to the creation of an art and architecture librarian's position to manage the Architecture Library with added duties in collection development for the areas of art, art history, and design. The author is the first librarian to occupy this redefined post.

Throughout the Architecture Library's history, gifts have helped to augment and enrich the collection. At times, they made up as much as 10 to 15 percent of total acquisitions. Gift books have their own intriguing stories, which chart the place of particular individuals in the University's history or illustrate the interests of certain benefactors. One of the most notable donors was Frank Lloyd Wright, who gave a copy of his Berlin-published *Ausgeführte Bauten und Entwürfe* after visiting the campus to discuss a possible master plan in 1922.[17] This handsome folio set is now considered one of the most important and valuable editions of Wright's work. In a similar spirit, Notre Dame graduate Ernest Graham of Graham, Anderson, Probst and White presented a portfolio of his firm's work to the library in 1934 after he completed the Hurley College of Commerce building. This volume has the added distinction of a beautifully engraved title page designed by Notre Dame alumnus James Canizaro, who had supervised the book's production in London.[18]

Individual gifts are tremendously useful, but libraries also need long-term endowments to support collection activities. The Architecture Library is fortunate to have three such funds: the Eli J. and Helen Shaheen Endowment for Italian and classical architecture, the Thomas and Anne Wamser Family Endowment for American architecture and, most recently, the Plym Endowment for vernacular and traditional architecture. These special funds support the purchase of current titles and rare or out-of-print material, providing necessary depth to important areas of the collection and commemorating distinguished friends and valued supporters of the school.

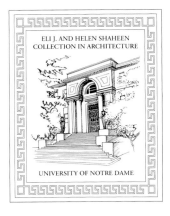

Figures 75 and 76.
Bookplates for the Shaheen and Wamser Endowments.

Figure 77.
The Rare Book Room,
1997.

  In 1995–97, extensive renovations to the building created a new library in the center of Bond Hall with its own rare book room. Under the leadership of architecture chairman Thomas Gordon Smith, two major gifts inaugurated the rare book collection. The Ryan family underwrote the acquisition of 74 titles from the Park List of architectural books known to have been in America before 1776. This exceptional donation was followed by a gift of some 250 titles from the Hitchcock List of American architecture books published from 1797 to 1895. Gwen and John Burgee and Mary O'Shaughnessy were the donors of this outstanding collection, which includes a fine second edition of the first American architectural book, Asher Benjamin's *The Country Builder's Assistant,* printed in 1798.

From its modest start 100 years ago, the Architecture Library today employs a staff of four, serves nearly 300 faculty and students and is housed in facilities that anticipate many years of growth. Its collection of 22,000 volumes reflects its beginnings in the Beaux-Arts tradition and its subsequent development into a true research library documenting architectural history, theory and practice. It is a mirror of the School of Architecture's own expansion as the curriculum evolved beyond the original vision of teaching what is not learned through professional practice to that of giving students a broad education in architecture and urbanism. The library holds both the literature that educated previous generations of architects and the evolving body of knowledge that will influence and form the architects of the future.

Figure 78.
The new Architecture Library, 1997.

■ ■ ■

ENDNOTES

1. Adolf K. Placzek, introduction to *Avery's Choice: Five Centuries of Great Architectural Books, One Hundred Years of an Architectural Library, 1890–1990* (New York: G.K. Hall, 1997), xxi.
2. Ibid., xxv.
3. *Catalogue of the University of Notre Dame* (1898–1899), 123.
4. *Bulletin of the University of Notre Dame* (1906–7), 86.
5. *Bulletin* (1923–24), 247.
6. Paul Foik, *University Library Annual Report* (1920–21).
7. Thomas Stritch, *My Notre Dame: Memories and Reflections of Sixty Years* (Notre Dame: University of Notre Dame Press, 1991), 116; Library Annual Report, 1924–25, [1] and 1925–26, 4.
8. *University Library Annual Report* 1928–29 and 1929–30.
9. *Bulletin* (1933–34), 233.
10. *University Library Annual Report* (1 July 1944–30 June 1945), 8–9.
11. Ida J. Bonicelli, *Report of the Architecture Library* (March 1947–June 1952).
12. Bonicelli, *A Report: The Architecture Library, University of Notre Dame* (29 March 1954).
13. New journals subscriptions included *Die Innenarchitektur, Kenchiku Bunka* [Architectural Culture], *Habitati: arquitectura e artes no Brasil, Chiesa e quartiere: quaderni di architettura sacra, Modulo: revista di arquitettura* and *Architectoniki. Acquisitions Department Report* 1957–58, 1958–59 and 1959–60, *Acquisitions Department Supplementary Report* (1 May–30 June 1959).
14. Tobi Milonadis, *Annual Report: The Architecture Library* (1964–1965).
15. Lawrence B. Anderson, "History's History" in *The Education of the Architect: Historiography, Urbanism, and the Growth of Architectural Knowledge, Essays Presented to Stanford Anderson*, ed. Martha Pollak (Cambridge: MIT Press, 1997), 440–41.
16. Jane C. Desmarais, *Report for the Engineering Library* (December 1938–July 1940), 7–9.
17. Letter from Frank Lloyd Wright to President Matthew J. Walsh, C.S.C., 13 December 1922. University Archives file UPWL 22/63.
18. *University Library Annual Report* (30 June 1934), 13; and interview with James Canizaro's son Robert Canizaro.

A Chronology of Important Events

1869

The first classes in architectural drawing and design are offered at Notre Dame.

1893

Father Andrew Morrissey, C.S.C., becomes University president.

1898

The degree program leading to a bachelor of architecture is established with Henry John Schlacks as director, assisted by Francis Xavier Ackerman.

1899

Eugenio P. Rayneri y Piedra of Havana, Cuba, enrolls in the program in December.

1904

Rayneri is the first graduate, receiving a bachelor of science in architectural engineering.

1905

Edward Rolland Adelsperger replaces Schlacks as director.

Father John W. Cavanaugh, C.S.C., becomes University president.

1906

The "Course in Architecture" is renamed the College of Architecture.

Spanish students Evaristo and Jose Batlle are the next to receive their degrees.

1909

Francis Wynn Kervick joins the architecture faculty.

1914

Adelsperger leaves and Kervick becomes acting director of the college.

1917

The Lemonnier Library by architect Edward Tilton opens.

1918

William Wirt Turner receives the first master's degree in architecture.

1919

Father James A. Burns, C.S.C., becomes University president.

1920

The College of Architecture becomes the Department of Architecture in the College of Engineering and Kervick is officially named chairman.

Vincent Fagan joins the faculty after receiving his bachelor of architecture from Notre Dame.

1922

Frank Lloyd Wright visits the campus to discuss a possible master plan.

Father Matthew J. Walsh, C.S.C., becomes University president.

1927

The department joins the Beaux-Arts Institute of Design (BAID).

1928

Father Charles L. O'Donnell, C.S.C., becomes University president.

1930

The department is admitted to membership in the Association of Collegiate Schools of Architecture.

1931

The department moves from the Main Building to Hoynes Hall, the former law school (now Crowley Hall), which is then named the Architecture Building.

1934

William Leo Newberry wins the BAID Warren Prize.

Father John F. O'Hara, C.S.C., becomes University president.

1939

Frank Montana joins the faculty.

1940

Father J. Hugh O'Donnell, C.S.C., becomes University president.

1945

The department wins the BAID medal for the school with the most BAID design problem awards in the previous year.

1946

Father John J. Cavanaugh, C.S.C., becomes University president.

An annex is added to the Architecture Building to house classrooms and the library.

1947

Ida Bonicelli is hired as the first professional architecture librarian.

1948

The five-year bachelor of architecture program replaces the previous four-year degree.

1949

The program is accredited by the National Architectural Accrediting Board.

1950

Francis Kervick steps down and Frank Montana is appointed chairman.

1952

Father Theodore M. Hesburgh, C.S.C., becomes University president.

1964

The department moves to the former Lemonnier Library after renovations designed by Montana and the library is renamed the Architecture Building.

1968

Patrick Horsbrugh creates the master's degree program in environic design.

1969

The Rome Studies Program is established with Otto Seeler as director.

1972

Ambrose Richardson is appointed chairman and Montana becomes director of the Rome Program.

Women students are admitted to Notre Dame for the first time.

1973

Mary Ann Proctor is the first female graduate.

1975

Michael A. Manfredi wins the Paris Prize.

1976

Otto Seeler starts his second term as Rome director.

1978

Robert L. Amico is recruited to chair the department.

1980

Frank Montana again serves as Rome director, retiring in 1986.

1982

The department becomes the School of Architecture within the College of Engineering.

1985

The rented Via Monterone facilities are purchased for the Rome Studies Center and inaugurated on January 16, 1986.

The endowed postgraduate degree program is established.

1986

Gloria Sama becomes Rome director.

1987

Father Edward A. Malloy, C.S.C., is named University president.

1989

Thomas Gordon Smith succeeds Amico as chairman.

1990

John W. Stamper is appointed Rome director.

1992

Robert Brandt launches the furniture design program.

1994

The school becomes independent of the College of Engineering and sets up its own advisory council.

1995

The school moves temporarily to the Hayes-Healy and Hurley buildings to prepare for renovations designed by Thomas Gordon Smith with architects of record Ellerbe Becket Associates.

1997

The Architecture Building is renamed Bond Hall in honor of benefactors William and Joanne Bond and inaugurated on March 21.

1998

Carroll William Westfall is appointed Frank Montana professor and chairman.

1999

Samir Younés is named Rome director.

Figure 79.
Vito Girone corrects a student's drawing, 1949.

Faculty Roster

University of Notre Dame
School of Architecture: 1898–1998

This roster of faculty was compiled from the University Catalogue *and* Bulletin *(1898–1998) and from the* College of Engineering Bulletin *(1940–79). The date next to each name is the year of first mention in the* Bulletin *or the year hired. Any omissions or inaccuracies reflect the information in these sources. Some names are spelled differently over time; however, the list shows the names as they most commonly appear in the sources noted. Part-time faculty members are not listed.*

In the case of early faculty and visiting faculty (designated as v), there are often no extant personnel files. Faculty members who taught both on the main campus and in Rome are listed only once in the main roster, rather than in both places. Similarly, professors who served only as chairman are listed once, but those who taught before or after their chairmanship are listed in the chairmen's roster as well as the teaching faculty roster. For more details on the individuals listed, contact the University of Notre Dame Archives.

Chairmen

Henry John Schlacks	1898–1905	Frank Montana	1950–72	Thomas Gordon Smith	1989–98
Edward Rolland Adelsperger	1905–13	Ambrose Richardson	1972–78	Carroll William Westfall	1998–
Francis Wynn Kervick	1914–50	Robert L. Amico	1978–89		

Teaching Faculty

Ackerman, Francis Xavier	1890	Crumlish, Brian J.	1964	Moore, William Smelsor	1943
Aime, Michel	1947	Deupi, Victor	1998 (v)	Morse-Fortier, Leonard	1988
Alhasani, Nadia M.	1991	Dodge, Raymond A.	1968	Moser, Brother Ferdinand, C.S.C.	1922
Amendola, Robert	1983 (v)	Doordan, Dennis P.	1990	Neff, Thomas K.	1977
Amico, Robert L.	1978	Economakis, Richard	1996	Nelson, Carl R.	1962
Ardito, David L.	1953	Emery, Elwood Allen	1903	Newberry, William Leo	1934
Bacon, Edmund N.	1983 (v)	Fagan, Vincent Francis	1921	Olgyay, Aladar	1947
Barrett, H. Stanford	1957	Featherstone, Kenneth A.	1961	Olgyay, Gyozo	1947
Beeby, Thomas H.	1983	Gabriel, J. Francois	1966	Pickard, Edward E.	1969
Bellalta, Esmee C.	1976	Girone, Vito Anthony	1945	Plati, Enrico	1972
Bellalta, Jaime J.	1976	Goeters, H.F.P.	1966	Richardson, Ambrose	1972
Bess, Philip H.	1990	Grillo, Paul J.	1952	Sacha, David W.	1979
Bieg, Harry	1929	Halas, Walter Henry	1920	Schultz, Robert J.	1950
Brandl, Ernest H.	1952	Hall, Spencer	1973	Seeler, Otto F.	1949
Brandt, Robert J.	1992	Horsbrugh, Patrick	1967	Selig, J. Daniel	1969
Brown, R. Gordon	1959	Hurtt, Steven	1973	Sherer, William Joseph	1946
Brubaker, Gerald Clement	1925	Jernegan Paul Frank	1946	Slade, Thomas	1971
Bullene, Rev. Richard S., C.S.C.	1993	Kervick, Francis Wynn	1909	Smith, Thomas Gordon	1989
Capek, Leslie	1982	Kleinman, Martin	1986 (v)	Sporleder, Donald E.	1963
Carroccia, Cara	1995	Kulski, Julian E.	1961	Sprague, Paul E.	1964
Chambers, Joseph J.	1993 (v)	Lay, Edmond Louis	1960 (v)	Stafford, Charles R.	1979
Chambers, Nancy Nerem	1992	Lykoudis, Michael N.	1991	Stamper, John W.	1984
Chang, I-Kwang	1994	McGraw, Joseph J.	1956	Stevens, Garry	1990
Christenson, Trace	1958	McHugh, John Wells	1945	Stoutenburg, William Jr.	1967
Craig, Brian K.	1977	Miller, John Edward	1932	Stroik, Duncan G.	1990
Crowe, Norman A.	1974	Montana, Frank	1939	Stuermer, Ray	1967

Teaching Faculty (continued)

Thoma, David	1976	Vitzthum, Sandra	1998	Williams, A. Richard	1981
Toperek, Walter J.	1965	Wesley, Richard H.	1981	Younés, Samir	1991
Turner, William Wirt	1936	Westfall, Carroll William	1998	Zerweck, Peter E.	1966 (v)
Ussner, Wilfred R.	1963				

Architecture Librarians

These names were compiled from library annual reports and the University Bulletin. *Any omissions reflect gaps in these sources. There were no architecture librarians before 1947.*

Bonicelli, Ida J.	1947
Coffman, Eleanor	1963
Curl, Sheila	1992
Decker, Geri	1965
Devine, Jane A. (architecture/art librarian)	1997
Havlik, Robert J. (engineering/architecture librarian)	1985
Kozak, Felice T.	1959
Masin, Anton C.	1984
Messersmith, Linda L. (branch supervisor)	1985
Milonadis, Tobi	1964
Sughroe, M. Patricia	1956
Webb, Deborah M. (branch supervisor)	1994

Rome Studies Center — 1969–98
Directors

Otto F. Seeler	1969–72
	1976–80
Frank Montana	1972–76
	1980–86
Gloria Lozano Sama	1986–90
John W. Stamper	1990–99

Teaching Faculty

Alexander, John	1997 (v)	Garrick, Jean Phillippe	1993 (v)	Rowe, Colin F.	1980 (v)
Baldauf, Hans R.	1991 (v)	Isreal, Franklin D.	1974 (v)	Rowland, Ingrid	1979 (v)
Barrett, Charles	1994 (v)	Lee, Jonathan	1995 (v)	Sacha, David W.	1979
Bernitsa, Petra	1991 (v)	Marder, Todd	1979 (v)	Sama, Gloria Lozano	1973
Bertoniere, John A.	1975	Martelli, Rev. Jose, C.S.C.	1982	Schumacher, Thomas L.	1981 (v)
Blanc, Francoise	1990 (v)	Mitrovic, Branko	1995 (v)	Sherwood, Roger D.	1982 (v)
Blanchard, Jeffrey	1979	Montgomery, Jason	1997 (v)	Steil, Lucien	1997 (v)
Burden, Jeffrey	1997 (v)	Negre, Valerie	1993 (v)	Tice, James T.	1981 (v)
Cameron, Richard W.	1990 (v)	Piccolo, Richard	1976	Van Lengen, Karen	1983 (v)
Craig, Peggy	1975 (v)	Pinto, John A.	1975 (v)	Wilson-Jones, Mark	1993 (v)
DiMaio, Judith	1979 (v)	Rajkovich, Thomas N.	1989 (v)		
Gamba, Evelyne	1974 (v)	Rosenshine, Matthew A.	1990 (v)		

Figure 80. (top)
Julian Kulski and students Anthony Mileto, Robert Canizaro, Jack Castin and John Martine review plans for a proposed redevelopment of downtown Michigan City, Indiana, 1962.

Figure 81. (bottom left)
Frank Montana, Kenneth Featherstone, Donald Sporleder and Brian Crumlish, c1968.

Figure 82. (bottom right)
Samir Younés and Norman Crowe discuss a housing project with students, 1998.

Graduates Roster

University of Notre Dame
School of Architecture: 1898–1998

The graduates roster was compiled from the University of Notre Dame official commencement programs and from alumni records. Any errors are unintended and reflect inaccuracies in these sources.

1904

Bachelor of Science in Architectural Engineering

Rayneri y Piedra, Eugenio P.
Havana, Cuba

1906

Bachelor of Science in Architectural Engineering

Batlle, Evaristo Ramon
Barcelona, Spain

Batlle, Jose Joaquin
Barcelona, Spain

1908

Bachelor of Science in Architecture

Adelsperger, Edward Rolland
South Bend, Indiana

1909

Bachelor of Science in Architecture

Carr, Henry William
Peoria, Illinois

1910

Bachelor of Science in Architecture

Walsh, George Patrick
Delphos, Ohio

1911

Bachelor of Science in Architecture

Helmkamp, William Bernard
Delphos, Ohio

1912

Bachelor of Science in Architecture

Kaiser, Benedict Joseph
South Bend, Indiana

Phillipps, Wendell Thomas
Milford, Massachusetts

1913

Bachelor of Science in Architecture

Tipton, William Reuben
East Las Vegas, New Mexico

Williams, Frederick
Wadena, Indiana

Bachelor of Science in Architectural Engineering

Baader, Ernest John
Chillicothe, Ohio

1914

Bachelor of Science in Architecture

Redden, William Joseph
Lewiston, Idaho

1915

Bachelor of Science in Architecture

Eck, Vincent John
Williamsport, Pennsylvania

Munger, Harold Henry
Perrysburg, Ohio

1916

Bachelor of Science in Architecture

Eckel, Jacob Edward
Syracuse, New York

Flynn, Joseph Patrick
Rochester, New York

Krajewski, Casimir Ignatiu
Chicago, Illinois

Turner, William Wirt
Washington, D.C.

1917

Bachelor of Architectural Engineering

Graham, Raymond John
Earlville, Illinois

Bachelor of Architecture

Campbell, John Bernard Jr.
Louisville, Kentucky

Trudelle, Matthew Eugene
Chippewa Falls, Wisconsin

1918

Bachelor of Architecture

Monning, Norbert Gerhardt
Chattanooga, Tennessee

Master in Architecture

Turner, William Wirt
Washington, D.C.

1919

Bachelor of Architecture

Blackman, Everett Augustus
Paris, Illinois

Carroll, Maurice John
Kansas City, Missouri

Conboy, Columbus
Alexandria, Indiana

McGarry, Bernard Clairvaux
Ashtabula, Ohio

1920

Bachelor of Architecture

Fagan, Vincent Francis
Hopedale, Massachusetts

Valker, Leo Irving
Hutchinson, Minnesota

Walsh, Vincent Hugh
Butte, Montana

Waters, Thomas Joseph
Westfield, Massachusetts

1921

Bachelor of Architecture

Conrad, Raymond John
Milwaukee, Wisconsin

Dollard, Thomas Vincent
Troy, New York

Miller, Callixtus Edwin
South Bend, Indiana

Rusche, Henry Joseph
Grand Rapids, Michigan

Bachelor of Architectural Engineering

McNamara, Edwin Lally
Cleveland, Ohio

1922

Degree of Architectural Engineer

Brubaker, Gerald Clement
Mishawaka, Indiana

Bachelor of Architecture

Behan, Joseph Bernard
Jackson, Michigan

Matthes, Walter John
South Bend, Indiana

Shaughnessy, Joseph Bernard
Kansas City, Kansas

Zwack, Clarence Anton
Dubuque, Iowa

1923

Degree of Architectural Engineer

Connell, John Francis
Denver, Colorado

Bachelor of Architecture

Chesnow, Louis
Detroit, Michigan

McHale, Thomas George
Fairbury, Nebraska

Moser, Brother
Ferdinand, C.S.C.
Notre Dame, Indiana

1924

Degree of Architectural Engineer

Geniesse, Levi Alphonse
Green Bay, Wisconsin

Gooley, Darrold Francis
South Bend, Indiana

Bachelor of Architecture

Cooke, Thomas Edward
Oak Park, Illinois

DeBarry, Charles Oscar
Lansing, Michigan

Noonan, Thomas Clifford
Ottawa, Illinois

1925

Bachelor of Architecture

Ambrose, Harry Morrison
Logan, Ohio

Bickel, Charles R.
Elkhart, Indiana

Dupay, Peter P.
Basking Ridge, New Jersey

Funk, Godfrey R.
Tucumcari, New Mexico

Mathey, Aloysius L.
Le Mars, Iowa

Mouch, Charles M.
Troy, Ohio

Rodighero, Rudolph George
Lockport, Illinois

Schomberg, Otto W.
Detroit, Michigan

1926

Bachelor of Architecture

McElroy, Wilbur
Norwalk, Connecticut

Nachtegall, Alfred Casper
Grand Rapids, Michigan

*Bachelor of Science in
Architectural Engineering*

Hall, Austin K.
Memphis, Tennessee

Johnson, Claude E.
Essex Junction, Vermont

1927

Bachelor of Architecture

Andrews, Frank Thomas
Cleveland, Ohio

Harwood, John Edward
Louisville, Kentucky

Worthington, Earl Carlton
South Bend, Indiana

1928

Bachelor of Architecture

Canizaro, James Thomas
Vicksburg, Mississippi

Duba, Silvin Peter
Libertyville, Illinois

Fettig, Leo Benedict
Chicago, Illinois

Ingram, James Maurice
Paducah, Kentucky

Knox, Robert Vincent
Terra Cotta, Illinois

Smith, David Henry
Chicago, Illinois

Sonnhalter, John Edward
Cleveland, Ohio

Thoma, Carl Arnold
Piqua, Ohio

*Bachelor of Science in
Architectural Engineering*

Bethke, Edward Joseph
Greene, Iowa

Brust, Paul Christopher
Milwaukee, Wisconsin

Schnurr, Alfred Anthony
Sandusky, Ohio

Varraveto, Patrick Michael
Chicago, Illinois

Worden, Roy Allan
South Bend, Indiana

1929

Bachelor of Architecture

Braeckel, Robert Joseph
Joplin, Missouri

Brysselbout, Paul Alphonse
Bay City, Michigan

Feldman, Maurice Anthony
Louisville, Kentucky

Horning, Claude H.
Akron, Ohio

Jewell, Everett Arnfield
South Bend, Indiana

Kreis, Donald Rudolph
Mishawaka, Indiana

Lauber, Joseph Wilton
South Bend, Indiana

Lushbaugh, Bernard Edward
South Bend, Indiana

O'Neill, John Patrick Jr.
Ogden, Utah

*Bachelor of Science in
Architectural Engineering*

Gorman, William Anthony
Bethlehem, Pennsylvania

Zimmerly, Richard Karl
South Bend, Indiana

1930

Bachelor of Architecture

Cook, Charles Oppenheimer
Bellevue, Ohio

Cotter, Laurens Paul
Buffalo, New York

Craddick, William Thomas
Rockford, Illinois

Farrell, Francis George
Pittsburgh, Pennsylvania

Gallagher, Arthur Joseph
Cleveland Heights, Ohio

Holland, Jerome Paul
Chicago, Illinois

Medland, Thomas Gallagher
Logansport, Indiana

Nolan, Stephen Patrick
Brooklyn, New York

Pahl, Charles Edward Jr.
Tiffin, Ohio

Smallwood, Charles Thomas
Chicago, Illinois

Zeedick, John George
Punxsutawney, Pennsylvania

*Bachelor of Science in
Architectural Engineering*

Drinane, Joseph Stephen
Englewood, New Jersey

Listzwan, Thomas
Proctor, Vermont

1931

Bachelor of Architecture

Alge, Robert Paul
Findlay, Ohio

Golobowski, Joseph Theodore
South Bend, Indiana

Hanson, John Henry
Fond du Lac, Wisconsin

Patrick, Andrew George
Bridgeport, Connecticut

West, Forrest Ross
South Bend, Indiana

*Bachelor of Science in
Architectural Engineering*

Brown, John Joseph
Central Falls, Rhode Island

Durbin, Clarence Arthur
LaPorte, Indiana

Marshall, Robert Maquire
Indianapolis, Indiana

Moller, Lawrence Frederick
Quincy, Illinois

Ridley, Walter Robert
Cleveland Heights, Ohio

Riedell, John Conrad
Paris, Illinois

1932

Bachelor of Architecture

Feely, Thomas Patrick
Joliet, Illinois

Hyland, Clifford Francis
Rockford, Illinois

Jauch, John William
Niles, Michigan

Kelly, Francis Joseph
Wilkes-Barre, Pennsylvania

Obelenus, Stanley Charles
Chicago, Illinois

Trolio, Peter John
Canton, Mississippi

*Bachelor of Science in
Architecture*

Galbraith, Thomas Paul
Gillespie, Illinois

Wieczorek, Edmund John
South Bend, Indiana

*Bachelor of Science in
Architectural Engineering*

Blommaert, Leonard Joseph
Chicago, Illinois

Cerri, William Taft
Mishawaka, Indiana

Davis, John William
Hazleton, Pennsylvania

Flanagan, Paul Edward
Grand Rapids, Michigan

Frank, Felix George
Maspeth, New York

Rodgers, Donald Clyde
Mishawaka, Indiana

Troost, Clarence Walter
Forest Park, Illinois

1933

Bachelor of Architecture

Chreist, Louis Ruben
South Bend, Indiana

De la Vergne, Jules Christian
New Orleans, Louisiana

Eppig, Arthur George
Wilmette, Illinois

Farrell, James Patrick
Green Bay, Wisconsin

Medland, Charles Joseph
Logansport, Indiana

Savage, Francis Hugh
Youngstown, Ohio

Stitt, Lawrence Joseph
Chillicothe, Ohio

Sullivan, John Joseph
Chicago, Illinois

*Bachelor of Science in
Architectural Engineering*

Byrne, Robert James
Norwich, New York

Dockendorff, Joseph Anton
LaCrosse, Wisconsin

Garrity, Donald Eugene
Chicago, Illinois

Heitger, Robert Harland
Bedford, Indiana

Malcolm, James Andrew
Fort Smith, Arkansas

Rigali, Paul Anthony
Oak Park, Illinois

1934

Bachelor of Architecture

Brust, John Joseph
Milwaukee, Wisconsin

Kelly, Richard Edward
Neenah, Wisconsin

Lavengood, Francis Leon
South Bend, Indiana

Newberry, William Leo
Alliance, Nebraska

Nortman, Harry Roder
Chicago, Illinois

Sausville, Clifford Francis
South Orange, New Jersey

*Bachelor of Science in
Architectural Engineering*

Fitzmaurice, Edward Joseph
Winchester, Indiana

Humbrecht, Henry Joseph
Fort Wayne, Indiana

Kellogg, Frederick Robert
Rock Springs, Wyoming

Sandmeier, Irwin Ernest
New Carlisle, Indiana

1935

Bachelor of Architecture

Hackenbruch, Arnold Charles
Milwaukee, Wisconsin

Kellogg, Frederick Robert
Rock Springs, Wyoming

Kohlman, Harold Louis
Elmhurst, Illinois

Tingley, John Kinney
Norwich, Connecticut

Wackerman, Adrian Joseph
Philadelphia, Pennsylvania

*Bachelor of Science in
Architectural Engineering*

Bernbrock, William Frederick
Aurora, Illinois

Gaul, Michael Felix
Chicago, Illinois

Hamm, Aaron John
Waverly, New York

Kellogg, Armand Wesley
Rock Springs, Wyoming

Love, Donald Wiley
Buffalo, New York

Morrison, Arnold Bernard
Rochester, New York

Rank, Gerald Thomas
River Forest, Illinois

1936

*Bachelor of Science in
Architecture*

Campbell, Charles Richard
Minneapolis, Minnesota

Creel y Lujan, Enrique
Mexico City, Mexico

Hertel, Morris Chester
South Bend, Indiana

Lee, John Michael
Salamanca, New York

McNeill, Fredolin Schlafly
Carlyle, Illinois

Nolen, James Aloysius
Philadelphia, Pennsylvania

*Bachelor of Science in
Architectural Engineering*

Beltemacchi, George Arthur
Logansport, Indiana

Hufnagel, Leon Clement
Clarion, Pennsylvania

Ott, Joseph Norbert
Quincy, Illinois

Palmer, Charles Carl
Mishawaka, Indiana

1937

Bachelor of Architecture

Hackner, John William
LaCrosse, Wisconsin

Van Namee, Albert Edmund
Bristol, Indiana

*Bachelor of Science in
Architectural Engineering*

McAuliffe, John Herbert
Oak Park, Illinois

Morrison, Reginald Alexander
Rochester, New York

1938

*Bachelor of Science in
Architecture*

Brown, Charles Matthew
Indianapolis, Indiana

Hoyos, Jaime Gomez
Manizales, Colombia

*Bachelor of Science in
Architectural Engineering*

Gerl, Richard Mathias
Manitowoc, Wisconsin

Halbert, Robert Thomas
Weedsport, New York

Hickey, Edward Thomas
Glen Ellyn, Illinois

Schumacher, Clarence Peter
Mishawaka, Indiana

Smith, Donald Hall
South Bend, Indiana

Sullivan, Robert Roger
Atlanta, Georgia

1939

*Bachelor of Science in
Architecture*

Hickey, Edward Thomas
Glen Ellyn, Illinois

1940

*Bachelor of Science in
Architecture*

Eilers, Bernard James
Rochester, New York

Gruenenfelder, Marcus Arthur
Highland, Illinois

Hennessy, Joseph Francis
Valley Stream, New York

Schultz, Robert Joseph
Oak Park, Illinois

1941

Bachelor of Architecture

McHugh, John Wells
Springfield, Ohio

Nolan, Robert Alexander
Louisville, Kentucky

Paskin, Milton
South Bend, Indiana

1942

Bachelor of Architecture

Bracke, Camiel Francis
East Moline, Illinois

Carney, John Bernard
Des Moines, Iowa

Gallagher, James Joseph
Schenectady, New York

Hackner, Robert Bernard
LaCrosse, Wisconsin

Haley, Douglas Francis
Gary, Indiana

Holland, Edward Lee
Morristown, New Jersey

Pfaller, Mark Arthur
Milwaukee, Wisconsin

Rossi, Ugo Dante
San Diego, California

Supplitt, George Louis
Riverside, Illinois

Whalen, Richard Thomas
Yonkers, New York

1943

Bachelor of Architecture

Andres, John Joseph
Hastings-on-Hudson,
New York

O'Connell, John Gabriel
Bridgeport, Connecticut

Sherer, Joseph John
West Hartford, Connecticut

Sherer, William Joseph
West Hartford, Connecticut

1944

Bachelor of Architecture

Sochalski, Edwin Stanley
Detroit, Michigan

*Bachelor of Science in
Architecture*

Cusick, Raymond Joseph
Jersey City, New Jersey

1945

Bachelor of Architecture

Cardenas, Jose Bernardo
Panama City, Panama

1946

Bachelor of Architecture

Delgado, Oscar Lupi
Caracas, Venezuela

Slater, Bernard James
Sharon, Pennsylvania

1947

Bachelor of Architecture

Bartolomeo, John Louis
Chicago, Illinois

Godollei, Paul Bary
South Bend, Indiana

Gonzalez, Ventura
Dallas, Texas

Grimaldi, Frank Virgil
Pittsburg, Kansas

Huelsbusch, Bernard Joseph
Effingham, Illinois

Lang, Joseph George
Pittsburgh, Pennsylvania

McGrath, Donald Joseph
St. Joseph, Michigan

Walsh, George Raymond
Canton, Ohio

Waterbury, Robert Harold
Skaneateles, New York

Zando, Raymond Joseph
War, West Virginia

1948

Bachelor of Architecture

Ardito, David Louis
Haworth, New Jersey

Bracken, Paul James
Johnstown, Pennsylvania

Braun, William James
University Heights, Ohio

Dinnen, James Michael
Fort Wayne, Indiana

Dodge, Charles Allen
Milwaukee, Wisconsin

Dwyer, Raymond William
Milwaukee, Wisconsin

Evans, John Martin
Detroit, Michigan

Griffin, Wlliam Francis
Bridgeport, Connecticut

Kress, James Joseph
Detroit, Michigan

Kruyer, Joseph Francis
South Bend, Indiana

Lugton, Charles Royall
Pine, Colorado

Mahoney, William Daniel
Denver, Colorado

Miller, Richard Paul
Elkhart, Indiana

Prokes, Francis Anthony
Jackson, Minnesota

Rigoni, Donald Leonard
Lockport, Illinois

Santarossa, Mario Carlo
Indianapolis, Indiana

Schubert, Lawrence James
South Bend, Indiana

Shiamanna, Lido Francis
San Francisco, California

Smith, Walter Wayne
Winona, Minnesota

Sosenheimer, John Louis
Fort Wayne, Indiana

Stolze, Alvin Keshner
Wood River, Illinois

Bachelor of Architectural Engineering

Haff, John Leater
West Frankfort, Illinois

1949

Bachelor of Architecture

Barber, Thomas Allan
Athens, Alabama

Barter, Frederick Gale
Rochester, Indiana

Benkowski, Anton Andrew
South Milwaukee, Wisconsin

Blomfield, Charles Alfred
San Antonio, Texas

Bourgeois, Eugene Paul
East Lynn, Massachusetts

Boyle, Vincent Taylor
Milford, Michigan

Carlson, Earl V. Jr.
Sheridan, Wyoming

Chopas, John
Haverhill, Massachusetts

Colon, Carlos Eduardo
Barranquitas, Puerto Rico

Donlon, Joseph Gerard
Chicago, Illinois

Dugan, Ross Francis Jr.
Idabel, Oklahoma

Gallaugher, Patrick Donavon
Lake Charles, Louisiana

Heck, Robert Warren
Council Bluffs, Iowa

Jones, Robert Lawton
McAlester, Oklahoma

Lieberenz, Robert LeVerne
Elkhart, Indiana

Marshall, Willoughby Marks
Apalachicola, Florida

McCarron, James Joseph III
Fort Wayne, Indiana

McGuire, Charles Edward
Indianapolis, Indiana

Moossy, Louis Emile
Shreveport, Louisiana

O'Brien, Daniel Curtis
New York, New York

Raley, Robert Lester
Wilmington, Delaware

Rammel, William Vance
Logansport, Indiana

St. Germain, John Henry
Montclair, New Jersey

Scibelli, Louis Antonio
Malden, Massachusetts

Spinney, Eric Don
Royal Oak, Michigan

Truemper, John William
Fort Wayne, Indiana

Van Ryn, Edwin Daniel
Detroit, Michigan

Ventura, August Francis
Jersey City, New Jersey

Weishapl, Patrick Joseph
Norfolk, Nebraska

Zekan, John David
Bridgeport, West Virginia

Bachelor of Architecture in Engineering

Black, Henry Chase
Battle Creek, Michigan

Cashin, Robert Charles
Stevens Point, Wisconsin

Hagedorn, James Henry
Chicago, Illinois

Kesting, James Bernard
Toledo, Ohio

Miller, Callix Edwin Jr.
South Bend, Indiana

Millin, Douglas Joseph
Chicago, Illinois

Oravec, Joseph Gregory
Sharon, Pennsylvania

St. Germain, John Henry
Montclair, New Jersey

Scibelli, Louis Antonio
Malden, Massachusetts

1950

Bachelor of Architecture

Andonian, David Aaron
Cleveland Heights, Ohio

Bauer, Edwin Richard
Mishawaka, Indiana

Bond, William West Jr.
Brownsville, Texas

Carvalho, Elmer Robert
Hilo, Hawaii

Company, Sebastian
Colon, Panama

Denning, Edward Patrick
Johnston, Rhode Island

Derbin, John
South Bend, Indiana

Drey, John Edmond
Des Moines, Iowa

Feifar, Theodore Andrew
Chicago, Illinois

Funk, Smith Adam
Chicago, Illinois

Gasparella, Joseph Richard
Vandergrift, Pennsylvania

Gustafson, Paul Nathan
Bemus Point, New York

Hiegel, Leo Joseph
Conway, Arkansas

Kirk, Richard Scott
Schenectady, New York

Koontz, William Donald
South Bend, Indiana

Kowalczyk, John Joseph
Brooklyn, New York

Lee, George Charles
South Bend, Indiana

Mathews, Joseph Louis
South Bend, Indiana

Mayotte, Bernard Joseph
Jackson, Michigan

McAlpine, Charles Frederick Jr.
Rochester, New York

Meek, Donald Ray
South Bend, Indiana

Moulton, Walter Redmond
Burlington, Vermont

Nemeth, Joseph Otto
Dayton, Ohio

Nilsen, Carl Henry
Westfield, Massachusetts

Nunnelley, William Allen
Louisville, Kentucky

O'Brien, Thomas Joseph
Davenport, Iowa

Omartian, Apkar Gabriel
Bronx, New York

Panzica, Anthony Joseph
South Bend, Indiana

Quinn, Harry Jeffers
Chicago, Illinois

Ruoff, William Joseph
St. Louis, Missouri

Schaaf, Norbert John
Jasper, Indiana

Tranter, Robert Davison
Middletown, Ohio

Vail, Thomas Augustine
South Amboy, New Jersey

Yarbro, Robert Lewis
Paducah, Kentucky

Bachelor of Architecture in Engineering

Laskowski, John Joseph
Buffalo, New York

Stechschulte, Russell Francis
Windber, Pennsylvania

Bachelor of Science in Architectural Engineering

Bruggeman, Arthur William
Fremont, Ohio

DeCrane, Vincent Francis
Cleveland Heights, Ohio

1951

Bachelor of Architecture

DeBruler, Robert Leslie
Indianapolis, Indiana

McAuliffe, Charles Michael
Bernardsville, New Jersey

Merrion, John Kelly
Chicago, Illinois

Moriarty, Robert Eugene
Great Falls, Montana

Munger, Harold Charles
Perrysburg, Ohio

Murphy, Charles Francis
Chicago, Illinois

Nachtegall, James Bernard
Grand Rapids, Michigan

Niephaus, Craig Arthur
St. Joseph, Michigan

See, John Jerome
Kansas City, Missouri

Walsh, William Hillsgrove
Concord, New Hampshire

Bachelor of Science in Architectural Engineering

Carr, Michael Martin
Indianapolis, Indiana

Nelson, Thomas Joseph Jr.
Utica, New York

Noetzel, Louis Sylvester
Detroit, Michigan

Rauth, Vincent Joseph
York, Nebraska

1952

Bachelor of Architecture

Castiello, Jaime Jose
Guadalajara, Mexico

Celento, Joseph Stephen
Canonsburg, Pennsylvania

Christen, Charles Lafayette
Pittsburgh, Pennsylvania

Daw, John Lawrence
Perry, Iowa

Heisler, Robert Paul
Richfield, Minnesota

Laffan, William Joseph
Kalamazoo, Michigan

Loosbrock, Thomas William
Charles City, Iowa

Tagawa, Walter Kazuhiko
Honolulu, Hawaii

Bachelor of Architecture in Engineering

McGuire, Joseph James
Indianapolis, Indiana

1953

Bachelor of Architecture

Angel, Joseph Martin
Toledo, Ohio

Baker, Richard Alden
San Diego, California

Bayless, Raymond Ellsworth Jr.
Oak Park, Illinois

Burgee, Joseph Zeno Jr.
Chicago, Illinois

Como, Elvio Carl
Aliquippa, Pennsylvania

Corker, Paul Dowd
Bradenton, Florida

Cushing, Paul Edward Jr.
Schenectady, New York

Dold, Robert Bruce
Glen Ridge, New Jersey

Eilers, Albert David
Deadwood, South Dakota

Emma, Thomas Alva
Geneva, Illinois

Hoffmann, Herman Albert
South Bend, Indiana

Joyce, Robert Francis
Scottsbluff, Nebraska

Little, Eugene Roland
Canton, Ohio

Lynch, John Patrick
Paterson, New Jersey

Lynch, Robert John
Winchester, Massachusetts

McManus, Joseph Warn
Battle Creek, Michigan

Mehoff, Boris Michael
Springfield, Ohio

Nagy, James Joseph
Detroit, Michigan

Nieman, Mark Allan
Columbus, Ohio

Noonan, Edward Joseph
Wilmette, Illinois

Prisco, Guy Vincent
Aurora, Illinois

Pugliano, Frederick Peter
West Springfield,
Massachusetts

Strickfaden, Roy James
Detroit, Michigan

1954

Bachelor of Architecture

Colavecchio, Louis Joseph
Hartford, Connecticut

Cuddihee, Donald Francis
St. Louis, Missouri

Farmer, William Douglas
South Bend, Indiana

Hausmann, Eugene Robert
Belleville, Illinois

Ingram, James Maurice
Louisville, Kentucky

Jaeger, Eugene George
Hammond, Indiana

Kane, William J. H.
Grand Ledge, Michigan

Karlsberger, Robert Louis
Columbus, Ohio

Kern, Herbert George
Erie, Pennsylvania

Kilian, John Joseph
Frankfort, Indiana

McCarthy, Edmund James
Larchmont, New York

Mirucki, Charles Joseph
Manchester, Connecticut

Montgomery, Robert Dickson
South Bend, Indiana

Muth, Albert Jerome
Columbus, Ohio

Petrillo, Joseph Angelo
Brooklyn, New York

Richmond, Victor James
Bradford, Pennsylvania

Saenz, Jaime Caicedo
Cali, Colombia

Saenz, Jaime Ignacio
Cali, Colombia

Savage, Joseph Richard Jr.
Canton, Ohio

Schwinn, Robert James
Cedar Rapids, Iowa

Stahl, Thomas Harmon
Madison, South Dakota

Sutton, Michael Charles
South Bend, Indiana

Trautman, Eugene Edward
Buffalo, New York

1955

Bachelor of Architecture

Aboitiz, Xavier Clausen
Cebu City, Phillipines

Balobeck, Joseph John Jr.
McKees Rocks, Pennsylvania

Boivin, Joseph Andre
Cohoes, New York

Brockway, Lee J.
Howe, Indiana

Campbell, Archie Reinald Jr.
Flint, Michigan

Cotleur, Thomas Edward
Brecksville, Ohio

Dwyer, William Rudolph
Waterbury, Connecticut

Ganther, Alfred Ray
Oshkosh, Wisconsin

Genovese, Anthony Vincent
Union City, New Jersey

Gulde, Charles James
Amarillo, Texas

Hinshaw, Donald Andrew
Indianapolis, Indiana

Hornak, James Anthony
Calumet City, Illinois

Kuskowski, Jerome Joseph
Milwaukee, Wisconsin

Lapasso, Anthony Charles
Chicago, Illinois

Malo, Edward Joseph
Chicago, Ilinois

Miller, David Francis
Rochester, New York

Percich, Angelo Anton
Rock Springs, Wyoming

Politzer, John Robert
Detroit, Michigan

Sawinski, Dennis Chester
Grand Rapids, Michigan

Shane, James Barry
Grosse Pointe Farms,
Michigan

Taylor, Ralph Vincent
Syracuse, New York

Valus, William Stephen Jr.
Stratford, Connecticut

Wallner, Robert George
Wauwatosa, Wisconsin

Welch, William Mack
Louisville, Kentucky

1956

Bachelor of Architecture

Alexander, Kay Edward
Wichita, Kansas

Behrmann, Donald Louis
Union City, New Jersey

Bretz, James Elmer
Springfield, Illinois

Brince, John Benedict
Albert Lea, Minnesota

Burgee, John Henry
Chicago, Illinois

Cahill, Thomas Aloysius
Gadsden, Alabama

Clemency, John Joseph
Brooklyn, New York

Cooke, Berkley Thomas
Trenton, Michigan

Driscoll, Jeremiah James
Congers, New York

Ferguson, Francis Lewis
National City, California

Gahl, Robert Allen
Wauwatosa, Wisconsin

Galehouse, Richard Frederick
Alliance, Ohio

Gallagher, David Reps
Parkersburg, West Virginia

Kern, Edward August
Erie, Pennsylvania

Landy, John William
Bronx, New York

Malesardi, Richard Thomas
Tenafly, New Jersey

Millmann, Charles Edward
Milwaukee, Wisconsin

Ochs, James Gerard
Evansville, Indiana

Pucillo, Anthony Mario
Mount Vernon, New York

Reilly, Paul Waldron
West Orange, New Jersey

Ronan, John Edward
Chicago, Illinois

Schenkel, James Joseph
Fort Wayne, Indiana

Schroeder, James Francis
Detroit Lakes, Minnesota

Shaughnessy, Joseph
Bernard Jr.
Kansas City, Missouri

Shepherd, John Barron
Milwaukee, Wisconsin

Simons, John Joseph Jr.
South Bend, Indiana

Van Besien, George Michael
Kansas City, Missouri

Villazon-Vazques, Manuel
Mexico City, Mexico

Ward, Joseph Alphonsus
Kirkwood, Missouri

1957

Bachelor of Architecture

Blank, Noel James
Toledo, Ohio

Bradtke, Philip Joseph
Chicago, Illinois

Burlage, James Edward
Fort Wayne, Indiana

Carissimi, Ronald Joseph
Sacramento, California

Chamorro, Eduardo
Managua, Nicaragua

Dyon, John Michael
Flushing, New York

Erdmann, Robert Louis
Milwaukee, Wisconsin

Fealy, Thomas Edwin
Franklin, Ohio

Funck, John Francis
Milwaukee, Wisconsin

Kelly, Edward Terrence
Laurelton, New York

Koester, Edward Charles
Wichita, Kansas

Linn, Robert Jeffery
Brooklyn, New York

Malaga, Guillermo Federico
Lima, Peru

Masini, Reno John
Chicago, Illinois

Nouhan, Robert George
Detroit, Michigan

Pattee, Francis William
Mason City, Iowa

Pierson, Maurice Albert
Managua, Nicaragua

Purucker, Ervin Frederick
South Bend, Indiana

Roney, Robert Francis
Detroit, Michigan

Schnurr, Ronald Alfred
Sandusky, Ohio

Smet, Ronald Edward
DePere, Wisconsin

Solomon, John Charles
Johnstown, Pennsylvania

Sweeney, James R.
Chicago, Illinois

Tardio, Felix
Canonsburg, Pennsylvania

Thole, William Louis
Summit, New Jersey

VanAuken, Richard Anthony
Shaker Heights, Ohio

Vrlich, Karl Marion
Gary, Indiana

Wiley, John Blaine
Toledo, Ohio

1958

Bachelor of Architecture

Antonelli, Felix Joseph Jr.
South Bend, Indiana

Asturias, Marco Vinicio
Guatemala City, Guatemala

Chiaro, John Joseph
River Forest, Illinois

Chihan, John Francis Jr.
Dearborn, Michigan

Cooke, James Thomas
Marinette, Wisconsin

Fabbro, Richard Arthur
Akron, Ohio

Flock, Donald Edward
Naperville, Illinois

Foran, David Anthony
Decatur, Illinois

Fuligni, Dante Paul
Rutherford, New Jersey

Harvey, John Armstrong
North Syracuse, New York

McCafferty, Charles Terrence
Grosse Pointe Park, Michigan

Mojzisek, George Ladislav
Belcamp, Maryland

Murphy, Martin Richard
Chicago, Illinois

Neubek, Frank Louis
Oaklawn, Illinois

Oddo, Jerome Bernard
Houston, Texas

Pruss, John Joseph
Seattle, Washington

Schmidt, Richard Karl
Grand Rapids, Michigan

Snyder, Daniel Ardellas
Convoy, Ohio

Wurzer, Thomas Duane
Rochester, New York

Zimmerman, Gary Vincent
Wauwatosa, Wisconsin

1959

Bachelor of Architecture

Amberg, Theodore Alfred
New Hyde Park, New York

Bertoncini, Gene Joseph
New York, New York

Cohan, Timothy Francis
Albany, New York

Dasek, John Joseph
Milwaukee, Wisconsin

Eckland, Robert Arthur
Moline, Illinois

Fournais, Eric Kund
Mexico City, Mexico

Gaudreau, William Lucius
Baltimore, Maryland

Gomez, Jose Maria
Juarez, Mexico

Hendrick, Lawrence Francis
Saginaw, Michigan

Hoffman, Robert Gene
Pontiac, Michigan

Kraemer, Kenneth Leo
Plain, Wisconsin

Kristopeit, Thomas Eugene
Davenport, Iowa

Lyne, Daniel Saindon
Chicago, Illinois

Moll, Donald Arthur
Brooklyn, New York

Molumby, Robert Eugene
Mount Prospect, Illinois

Motter, Michael Adam
Canton, Ohio

Paiewonsky, Benjamin
Dominican Republic

Pezzuti, Thomas A.
Camp Hill, Pennsylvania

Rossi, John Joseph
Chicago, Illinois

Saksefski, Gervase Cyril
Milwaukee, Wisconsin

Schafer, William Murray
Akron, Ohio

Scheuermann, Franz Peter
Westfield, New Jersey

Schoeneman, Robert Barton
Hawarden, Iowa

Schonbachler, Loran Denis
Napanoch, New York

Shank, Edwin Gerald Jr.
Winamac, Indiana

1960

Bachelor of Architecture

Becker, Robert George
Cleveland, Ohio

Callahan, Michael Thomas
Hillsdale, Michigan

Eberl, David Eugene
Buffalo, New York

Fowler, James Alan
Bismarck, North Dakota

Garza, Sergio Hector
Mexico City, Mexico

Gattozzi, Pasqual Anthony
Lyndhurst, Ohio

Gurdian, Alvaro Manuel
Managua, Nicaragua

Howell, James Harold
Muskegon, Michigan

Kane, Patrick Francis
Sherman Oaks, California

Kelly, Michael Daniel
Menlo Park, California

Lacz, Stanley John
Paterson, New Jersey

Lazor, John Basil
Chagrin Falls, Ohio

Miller, James Wallace
Park Forest, Illinois

Noll, Charles Edward
McCook, Nebraska

Osorio, Peter Ivan
Managua, Nicaragua

Parker, Ronald Lee
Burbank, California

Penalba, Edgar Jose
Managua, Nicaragua

Petrungaro, Charles Eugene
Chicago, Illinois

Quinn, Thomas Patrick
Chicago, Illinois

Rodriguez, Joseph Priede
Tampa, Florida

Ronchelli, Edward Orlando
Santa Rosa, California

Thrall, William Francis
Grand Rapids, Michigan

Victor, Gary Miles
Tulsa, Oklahoma

Walter, Daniel Francis
Birmingham, Michigan

1961

Bachelor of Architecture

Cividin, Glen Eugene
Trail, Canada

Da Silva, Peter Nolasco
Manila, Philippines

Dragos, Stephen Francis
Lyons, Illinois

Farina, Thomas Anthony
Newark, New Jersey

Gaio, Raymond Lee
Springfield, Illinois

Gimber, Douglas Alan
Los Angeles, California

Hamilton, John Patrick
Marion, Indiana

Hiegel, Andrew Peter
Conway, Arkansas

Jankowski, Conrad Chester
South Bend, Indiana

Kelly, Dennis Jerome
Summit, New Jersey

Korbuly, Laszlo J.
South Bend, Indiana

Kostecky, John Michael Jr.
Akron, Pennsylvania

Lamb, Thomas Joseph
Chicago, Illinois

Landry, John Phillips
Bloomfield Hills, Michigan

Legan, Joseph Robert Jr.
Joliet, Illinois

Miro, Antonio R.
Rio Piedras, Puerto Rico

Oxley, George Kenneth Jr.
Detroit, Michigan

Quinn, Richard Walter
New Britain, Connecticut

Seckler, Arthur Jerome
New York, New York

Sterling, Walter Patrick
South Bend, Indiana

Summers, Luis Henry
Lima, Peru

Walwood, Richard H.
Milton, Massachusetts

1962

Bachelor of Architecture

Boldrick, Charles C.
Lebanon, Kentucky

Canizaro, Robert Host
Jackson, Mississippi

Cassidy, James Patrick
Larchmont, New York

Castin, John Arnold
Okmulgee, Oklahoma

Duffy, Edward J.
Northport, New York

Dunne, James Richard
Bay Shore, New York

Earthman, John Alfred
Houston, Texas

Fitzgerald, James Thomas
Dayton, Ohio

Giattina, Joseph Paul Jr.
Birmingham, Alabama

Graf, Werner Herman
Michigan City, Indiana

Kratt, William Joseph
South Bend, Indiana

Maniatis, Theodore Paul
Chicago, Illinois

Martine, John Anthony
Monroeville, Pennsylvania

Mileto, Anthony Michael
Baltimore, Maryland

Murphy, Paul Michael
Wilmette, Illinois

Rauch, Bernard Francis
Fort Wayne, Indiana

Regan, Thomas Edward Jr.
Oil City, Pennsylvania

Trigiani, David Michael
Bangor, Pennsylvania

1963

Bachelor of Architecture

Battle, David George
Missoula, Montana

Cooper, Carlisle Edward
Webster Groves, Missouri

DesRochers, Paul Valere
Wilmington, Delaware

Donnelly, Edward Owen
Waltham, Massachusetts

Doyle, Peter Gerald
Beaumont, Texas

Enright, Stephen Luke
Winchester, Massachusetts

Fay, William Jerome
Hollywood, California

Gemperle, Albert Rich Jr.
Red Bank, New Jersey

Gill, Denis Peter
Rocky River, Ohio

Green, Robert Alfred Jr.
Pleasantville, New York

Grusdis, Richard John
Steger, Illinois

Haffey, Sam Anson
Lyndhurst, Ohio

Highfield, William Benjamin Jr.
South Bend, Indiana

Hoffmann, Robert Edward
Chicago, Illinois

Huiskamp, James Edward
Keokuk, Iowa

Maersch, Francis Carl
Sheboygan, Wisconsin

Myles, Michael Joyce
Chappell, Nebraska

Patout, Frank William
Navasota, Texas

Ricca, Thomas David
Pittsburgh, Pennsylvania

Roake, Stephen Allen
Great Neck, New York

Studebaker, Ira John
Belmond, Iowa

Taylor, Robert John
Westfield, New Jersey

Weis, Thomas Joseph
Louisville, Kentucky

1964

Bachelor of Architecture

Boylan, John Joseph Jr.
Jersey City, New Jersey

DeBartolo, Michael James
Youngstown, Ohio

Donahue, Dennis Martin
East Hartford, Connecticut

Dwyer, Thomas Alexander
Grafton, Wisconsin

Feske, Carl David
Indianapolis, Indiana

Gallagher, Daniel Patrick
Mason City, Iowa

Lawless, Robert Edward III
Greenwich, Connecticut

Leader, John Thomas
South Bend, Indiana

Lorr, John Francis
Brookfield, Illinois

Martinez, Raul
San Juan, Puerto Rico

Morford, John Edward
Decatur, Illinois

Newlove, Victor Melvin
Santa Monica, California

Nolan, Thomas Jerome
Louisville, Kentucky

Nolen, James Aloysius III
Philadelphia, Pennsylvania

Weinmann, Raymond Ludwig
Huntingdon Valley,
Pennsylvania

Yosten, Bernard Matthew
West Point, Nebraska

1965

Bachelor of Architecture

Anella, Stephen Anthony
New Milford, New Jersey

Apostolou, Paul Charles
Pittsburgh, Pennsylvania

Childs, James Elsworth
Tipton, Indiana

Cittadine, Gerald Joseph
South Bend, Indiana

Connelly, Thomas Augustine
St. Louis, Missouri

Davis, John Butler
Harrisburg, Pennsylvania

Di Vito, Pasquale Frank
Chicago, Illinois

Gillan, John Joseph
River Edge, New Jersey

Hricko, James John
Torrington, Connecticut

Hynes, Richard William
Hinckley, Illinois

Kolasinski, Daniel Edwin
Toledo, Ohio

Kuhns, Thomas Joseph
Aurora, Illinois

Long, Paul Thomas
Harrisburg, Pennsylvania

Marro, Michael Francesco
Cranston, Rhode Island

McHugh, Thomas William
Leominster, Massachusetts

Newberry, Norman Richard
Hollywood, California

Stegich, Steve Richard III
Little Falls, New York

Twohig, Philip James
Fond du Lac, Wisconsin

Uribe, Jorge Humberto
Medellin, Colombia

Van De Walle, John Charles
Sioux Falls, South Dakota

Waite, Patrick Michael
Milwaukee, Wisconsin

1966

Bachelor of Architecture

Bairley, Daniel Raymond
Monroe, Michigan

Beringer, David John
Bellwood, Nebraska

Butot, Luis Frederik Johannes
Curaçao, Netherlands
Antilles

Ching, Francis Dai-Kam
Honolulu, Hawaii

Darin, Joseph
Glendale, California

Dobie, John Edward
Boston, Massachusetts

Eiben, Michael Robert
Lebanon, Pennsylvania

Girardi, Maurice Vincent
Memphis, Tennessee

Holzheimer, Gerald Thomas
Cleveland, Ohio

Hunt, Richard Russell
Woonsocket, Rhode Island

Kasprisin, Ronald Joseph
Cleveland, Ohio

McDermott, John James
College Point, New York

McManus, James Michael
Syracuse, New York

Pastor, Frank James
Manhasset, New York

Pfliegel, J. Thomas
Cincinnati, Ohio

Powers, Dennis Edward
New York, New York

Powers, Stephen Thomas
Chicago, Illinois

Roman, Roque Arturo
Mayaguez, Puerto Rico

Roughgarden, Richard Joseph
Hawthorne, New Jersey

Staub, John Thomas
Chicago, Illinois

Torres, Luis Antonio
Rio Piedras, Puerto Rico

Torti, John Francis
White Plains, New York

1967

Bachelor of Architecture

Belliveau, Paul Randle
Fitchburg, Massachusetts

Bodnar, Robert David
Pittsburgh, Pennsylvania

Cardenal, Alejandro
Managua, Nicaragua

Connolly, William Mark
New Brunswick, New Jersey

Donohue, William Richard
Nutley, New Jersey

Fiory, Richard Theodore
Lebanon, New Jersey

Gardner, Kevin Gerard
Neponsit, New York

Gurchik, Robert Joseph
Elyria, Ohio

Hanafin, Richard Brian
Wenham, Massachusetts

Harmicar, Robert Michael
Youngstown, Ohio

Humphries, John Francis Jr.
Dallas, Texas

Kammerer, Edward Joseph
South Bend, Indiana

Keefe, Dennis Harry
West Roxbury,
Massachusetts

Kozdras, Richard Francis
Hammond, Indiana

McArdle, Edward Gerald Jr.
Fort Wayne, Indiana

Meinert, Edward Glenn
Pittsburgh, Pennsylvania

Mylan, Dennis Allen
Dumont, New Jersey

Nelson, Benjamin Edmund
Chicago, Illinois

Overly, Orbie Ross
Kansas City, Missouri

Rutter, Ralph Frederick
Hailey, Idaho

Scheideman, Edward Smith
Solon, Ohio

Smith, Michael Edward
Omaha, Nebraska

Snider, Douglas Shannon
Medford, Oregon

Velleco, James Anthony
Cranston, Rhode Island

Walthers, Bruce Julius
Milwaukee, Wisconsin

1968

Bachelor of Architecture

Bender, Stephen Otto
Alexandria, Indiana

Chelminiak, Paul Leon
Seattle, Washington

Clasby, Thomas Vincent
Ipswich, Massachusetts

Duffy, James Thomas
Doylestown, Pennsylvania

Duffy, Robert Kendall Jr.
Grand Rapids, Michigan

Dyson, Robert L.
Elmwood Park, Illinois

Erbach, Gerald George
Mount Prospect, Illinois

Florestano, Dana Joseph
Indianapolis, Indiana

Hee, Lawrence Yau Sung
Honolulu, Hawaii

Lesperance, William Glenn
Essexville, Michigan

Luby, John Martin
Dallas, Texas

Lynch, James Christopher
Oradell, New Jersey

Martino, Anthony Chester
Utica, New York

Maves, John Howard
Grand Forks, North Dakota

Mulvihill, Stephen Roy
Kankakee, Illinois

Murray, Francis O'Brien
Newburyport, Massachusetts

Rechtsteiner, Steven Allen
Cincinnati, Ohio

Reddy, Martin Joseph
Birmingham, Michigan

Sieks, Melvin Joseph
Peoria, Illinois

Widdifield, Alvie George Jr.
San Antonio, Texas

1969

Bachelor of Architecture

Balich, George Thomas
North Reading,
Massachusetts

Barbosa-Jerez, Jose E.
San Juan, Puerto Rico

Bellini, Enrique Arturo
Charlotte Amalie,
St. Thomas

Bosco, Joseph Salvatore
Prospect, Connecticut

Brandmeier, Philip August
Rochester, New York

Butz, Richard Louis
Eaton, Ohio

Canestaro, James Carmen
Cortland, New York

Clasby, Thomas Vincent
Ipswich, New York

Corrado, Patrick George
Port Jervis, New York

Drnevich, Richard Paul
North Versailles,
Pennsylvania

DuCharme, Alvin Joseph
Sunol, California

Genis, Thomas Peter
Gardner, Massachusetts

Graham, Charles George
Charleston, South Carolina

Green, William Joseph
Arlington, Massachusetts

Hafel, Robert John
Springfield, Illinois

Kachik, James Richard
Hockessin, Delaware

Kearney, Daniel Theodore
Palos Park, Illinois

Kulcsar, Stephen Joseph Jr.
Barberton, Ohio

Livingston, Byron Naylor
Omaha, Nebraska

Lontai, Adam Almos
South Bend, Indiana

Melone, Ralph Joseph
Mount Top, Pennsylvania

Munsch, Harold Michael
Houston, Texas

Orloff, Joseph Carl
Bloomfield Hills, Michigan

Perkins, James Reimer
Oconomowoc, Wisconsin

Steinhauser, Ralph Louis
Louisville, Kentucky

Wilks, Robert Charles
Westlake, Ohio

Wright, Stephen Thedieck
Sidney, Ohio

1970

Bachelor of Architecture

Anderson, Neil Bernard
Aurora, Illinois

Barker, Gary Alvin
Billings, Montana

Cody, Patrick Joseph
Chicago, Illinois

Crawford, Patrick William
Bowie, Maryland

Czekanski, Antoni Robert
Westmont, New Jersey

DiSabatino, E. John
Wilmington, Delaware

Fitzpatrick, John Andrew
Linden, New Jersey

Fravel, William Edward Jr.
Santa Cruz, California

Gmitter, Donald Alan
Mt. Lebanon, Pennsylvania

Harrison, Michael Thomas
Miami, Florida

Hartman, Robert Richard
Madison, New Jersey

Kelliher, James Matthew
Westwood, Massachusetts

Mangan, Michael Daniel
Forest City, Iowa

McCarthy, Patrick William
Youngstown, Ohio

Moriarity, Peter Henkels
Pittsburgh, Pennsylvania

Rockhill, Daniel
Bethpage, New York

Role, Raymond Edward
Chicago, Illinois

Russell, Daniel Louis
Douglaston, New York

Schmitt, Charles Leo
Pittsburgh, Pennsylvania

Shern, John William
Brookfield, Wisconsin

Skarstein, Ole Bernt
Mo Rana, Norway

Tarkington, Harold Wade
Greenwich, Connecticut

Torborg, Ronald David
Fort Wayne, Indiana

Valenta, Glenn Stanley
Allendale, New Jersey

Wachtel, James Maurice
Donelson, Tennessee

Wolnitzek, Frederick
William III
Fort Wright, Kentucky

1971

Bachelor of Architecture

Azizi, Enver
San Juan, Puerto Rico

Bajandas, Robert William
Louisville, Kentucky

Beyer, William Dennis
Alexandria, Virginia

Bono, Richard J.
Bronx, New York

Borger, Thomas J.
Elkhart, Indiana

Braley, Scott William
Indianapolis, Indiana

Brown, David Charles
Edin, New York

Burkavage, William Joseph Jr.
Springfield, Pennsylvania

Buscanics, Robert Francis
Belle Vernon, Pennsylvania

Cassiere, Joseph Louis II
Shreveport, Louisiana

Cheney, Frank Reuter
Kenmore, New York

Chmura, Jeffrey Alan
Pawtucket, Rhode Island

Clifford, Thomas David
Holliston, Massachusetts

Diefenbach, Donald James
Woodbridge, Virginia

Doolan, James Joseph Jr.
Boston, Massachusetts

English, Jerome Robert
Gillette, New Jersey

Gallegos, Phillip Benitez Jr.
Pueblo, Colorado

Germano, Louis Michael
Melrose Park, Illinois

Johnston, Jeffrey F.
Syracuse, New York

Jones, Samuel Francis
Marion, Indiana

Kearns, Thomas James
Downey, California

Kirstoff, Kim Charles
Hampton, Virginia

LeDuc, Evan Martin
Decatur, Michigan

Leonardo, Ernest Joseph
Vineland, New Jersey

Liebner, Frank Anthony
Chicago, Illinois

Lopez-Molne, Roberto Rafael
South Bend, Indiana

Madej, Gregory Paul
Monongahela, Pennsylvania

Manning, John Joseph Jr.
Worcester, Massachusetts

Marin, Carlos Jose
Lima, Peru

Pennell, Russell Anthony
Neptune, New Jersey

Peters, William Albert Jr.
Stamford, Connecticut

Ponko, William R.
Merrill, Wisconsin

Schmitz, Andrew Joseph III
Huntington, New York

Smith, Michael Woodrow
Peru, Illinois

Suzuki, Edward
Tokyo, Japan

Tierney, Gary Michael
Orange, Connecticut

Troyer, LeRoy S.
South Bend, Indiana

Wickstrom, Douglas M.
Michigan City, Indiana

Winkel, Matthew John Jr.
Hayden, Arizona

1972

Bachelor of Architecture

Barlo, Paul Leonard
Hillside, New Jersey

Bemis, William Robert
Brookfield, Wisconsin

Blake, Michael Edward
Montvale, New Jersey

Brakalov, Ted Khristov
Pittsburgh, Pennsylvania

Chiavaroli, Julius Joseph
Rochester, New York

Coleman, Mark Elliott
Cleveland, Ohio

Cox, Brian Michael
Houston, Texas

Dennis, Christopher Kevin
Albany, New York

Fairbrother, John Henry III
West Hartford, Connecticut

Hatke, Eugene Robert
Lafayette, Indiana

Hubbard, Mark Owen
Middlefield, Connecticut

Hunter, Stephen Clay
Sikeston, Missouri

Jones, Mark David
Rolling Prairie, Indiana

Kuhn, John Wood Jr.
Garden City, New York

Lemick, Michael Charles
Dyer, Indiana

Liscano, Michael Andrew
Columbus, Ohio

Maguire, John Patrick
Philadelphia, Pennsylvania

McCleer, Michael Joseph
Jackson, Michigan

McCormack, Ricardo Jorge
Miami, Florida

Mitchell, Robert Dudley
Levittown, New York

Noe, Robert Joseph
Swanton, Ohio

Schneider, Philip James
Babylon, New York

Seiter, Jeffrey Christopher
Xenia, Ohio

Short, Terrance Joseph
South Bend, Indiana

Spurr, Randall Alan
St. Louis, Missouri

Van Dyk, Peter Martin
Santa Rosa, California

Weiler, Charles Joseph
Maplewood, New Jersey

1973

Bachelor of Architecture

Anderson, Richard Pershing
Oak Lawn, Illinois

Anthony, Mark Joseph
Troy, New York

Antinozzi, Daniel Paul III
Stratford, Connecticut

Barbieri, Louis Edward
Metuchen, New Jersey

Borawski, Thomas John
Simsbury, Connecticut

Borg, Stephen W.
South Bend, Indiana

Brockman, Patrick
Fort Madison, Iowa

Brown, William V.
Broomall, Pennsylvania

Cahill, Gregory Ferris
Pacific Palisades, California

Casper, Michael Owen
Milwaukee, Wisconsin

Cerreta, Dennis Michael
Sea Girt, New Jersey

Clemency, William Marshall
Mendham, New Jersey

Colella, Pasquale Vincent
New York, New York

DeBarbieri, James Edward
Nutley, New Jersey

DeSapio, James Luciano
Baptistown, New Jersey

Devlin, Joseph David
Ramsey, New Jersey

Donahue, James Franci
Decatur, Georgia

Doozan, Carl William Jr.
Saginaw, Michigan

Dunn, Christopher Charles
North Haven, Connecticut

Fox, John Jay III
Chicago, Illinois

Germano, Anthony Joseph
Mishawaka, Indiana

Gick, Michael Morgan
Fowler, Indiana

Illig, Robert John Jr.
Erie, Pennsylvania

Kelly, Michael J.
Chicago, Illinois

King, Charles Anthony
Wheaton, Illinois

Kuna, John Joseph
Carbondale, Pennsylvania

Liddy, Charles Darrel
Minneapolis, Minnesota

Madel, Douglas Martin
Glen Ellyn, Illinois

Mastin, William Duffy Jr.
Chattanooga, Tennessee

McQuilkin, John Joseph
Chattanooga, Tennessee

Minch, David John
Cleveland, Ohio

Moran, John Fahey
Massapequa, New York

Murray, Christopher
Charles III
Hempstead, New York

Musica, Frank Dominic
Meadville, Pennsylvania

Peine, John George Jr.
Davenport, Iowa

Proctor, Mary Ann
Cleveland, Ohio

Ruiz, Hector Miguel
Jackson Heights, New York

Schreckengast, Stewart Wayne
Lafayette, Indiana

Senff, Arlen Ray
Bremen, Indiana

Smith, Sherman Wayne
Winona, Minnesota

Studenic, William Jr.
Norton, Ohio

Velez, Jose
Jackson Heights, New York

Zapor, Lester John
Weirton, West Virginia

1974

Bachelor of Architecture

Alicandro, Stephen Brent
Shrewsbury, Massachusetts

Aulisio, Jerome Joseph
Youngstown, Ohio

Bunster, Max
Miami, Florida

Carpentier, Diane Marie
Grosse Pointe Farms,
Michigan

Cooper, Mark Anthony
Cincinnati, Ohio

DeFrees, Alan Robert
Florissant, Missouri

Dunne, Timothy Richard
Troy, New York

Eddy, Stephen Joseph
Geneva, New York

Fodness, David Allan
South Bend, Indiana

Fronczak, David
Gary, Indiana

Gibbons, Richard Alan
Maumee, Ohio

Grant, Ronald Archibald
Kingston, Jamaica

Grau, Philip August III
Milwaukee, Wisconsin

Hafner, Joseph Cabrini
Detroit, Michigan

Knevel, Kenneth Michael
North Lafayette, Indiana

Lester, Michael Scott
Midland, Michigan

McDonough, Michael Patrick
Bennington, Vermont

McGuire, Louis Patrick Jr.
Wisner, Nebraska

Merighi, Lawrence Joseph
Vineland, New Jersey

Miller, Timothy Eugene
Elkhart, Indiana

O'Connor, Thomas Joseph
Drexel Hill, Pennsylvania

Pfaller, Mark Frank
Elm Grove, Wisconsin

Riebschlegar, David George
Saginaw, Wisconsin

Rupar, Kenneth Francis
Timonium, Maryland

Shea, Brian John
Quincy, Massachusetts

Snell, Ralph William
Amsterdam, New York

Suhre, David Court
Batesville, Indiana

Sykes, Thomas
Margate, New Jersey

Tritschler, Gerald Joseph
Westlake, Ohio

Weber, George Frederick
William III
South Bend, Indiana

Whitecotton, Michael Gilbert
New Ross, Indiana

1975

Bachelor of Architecture

Aleci, Eugene Laurence
Bradford, Pennsylvania

Bates, William Jerome
Canonsburg, Pennsylvania

Boyd, Hugh Alan
Stoneham, Massachusetts

Brezina, Carlos George
Newark, Ohio

Bridges, James Paul
Pavilion, New York

Bryant, Michael J.
Cincinnati, Ohio

Burke, Thomas Edmund
Los Gatos, California

Casaccio, Lee Alfred
Havertown, Pennsylvania

Chang, Paul Francis Xavier
Kingston, Jamaica

Clitheroe, Herbert Charles Jr.
Anaheim, California

Clynne, Martin Stuart
Brigantine, New Jersey

Conley, Lawrence Emerson
Rockville, Maryland

Coppinger, Michael T.
Cincinnati, Ohio

De Candia, Michael John
Brooklyn, New York

Deml, Robert John
Washington, Pennsylvania

Epping, Randy Charles
Salem, Oregon

Fitzgerald, Edward Lisle
Scarsdale, New York

Foglia, William Stephen
Pittsburgh, Pennsylvania

Foley, Kenneth James
South Bend, Indiana

Fordonski, Michael Joseph
Matteson, Illinois

Gangotena, Enrique
Quito, Ecuador

Halpin, James Patrick
Alexandria, Virginia

Hobbs, John Charles
Hamilton, Ohio

Jochems, John Leonard
Wichita, Kansas

Joyce, William Patrick Jr.
Pittsburgh, Pennsylvania

Kirkpatrick, Richard David
Glenside, Pennsylvania

Kubik, Matthew
Michigan City, Indiana

Kuspan, Joseph Francis
Struthers, Ohio

Lampkin, Mary Martha
Decatur, Illinois

Manfredi, Michael A.
Rockville, Maryland

Manuel, Juan
Beltranena Orive, Guatemala

McDonald, Michael W.
Milwaukee, Wisconsin

Melhado, Carlos Armando
Linares
Santa Ana, El Salvador

Morrison, John Thomas
Rochester, New York

Moylan, Stephen Craig
Chicago, Illinois

Mudd, Edward Ralston
Baltimore, Maryland

O'Brien, James Edward
Rockville, Maryland

O'Hora, Maureen Ann
Midland, Michigan

Parme, Robert Jeffrey
La Jolla, California

Plennert, John R.
Chicago, Illinois

Raih, Daniel J.
Freeport, Illinois

Ramentol, James John Jr.
Union, New Jersey

Reuther, John Michael
Muncy, Pennsylvania

Rivera, Miguel Antonio
Santa Ana, El Salvador

Rodriguez, Roland V.
San Antonio, Texas

Sabonge, Rafael Feniel
Panama City, Panama

Schute, Valentine Joseph Jr.
Doylestown, Pennsylvania

Sholl, David John
Fort Wayne, Indiana

Thoma, David N.
Des Plaines, Illinois

Waldock, Leland James
Olean, New York

Wentling, James Walter
Lancaster, Pennsylvania

Weyland, Charles William Jr.
Louisville, Kentucky

Wurst, James Philip
Miami, Florida

Younger, Michael Gerard
Helena, Montana

Zielonko, Thomas Alexander
Troy, Illinois

1976

Bachelor of Architecture

Acker, Richmond Paul
East Grand Rapids, Michigan

Barringer, Robert Stewart
Des Peres, Missouri

Benz, Gregory Paul
Bethlehem, Pennsylvania

Blitch, Ronald Buchanan
New Orleans, Louisiana

Brooks, James Herbert
Elmsford, New York

Bullene, Richard Stanley Jr.
Salinas, California

Carter, William Daniel
Trafford, Pennsylvania

Coogan, Charles Christopher
Houston, Texas

Cramer, Arthur James Jr.
West Springfield, Virginia

Davidson, Robert Whelan
Durham, North Carolina

Dengler, John Joseph III
Littleton, Colorado

Duber, Allan Joseph
Avon Lake, Ohio

Dye, Williston Lamar Jr.
Bethesda, Maryland

Fiala, Robert Arthur
Garfield Heights, Ohio

Fox, James Anthony
Chicago, Illinois

Fratti, Robert Carl
East Detroit, Michigan

Funk, Susan Karen
Tampa, Florida

Godfrey, William Riehle
Orchard Park, New York

Greenburg, Ann Elizabeth
Wingate, Indiana

Hadley, Terry Ben
Bethesda, Maryland

Herr, Mark C.
Elm Grove, Wisconsin

Hoerstman, Thomas Alan
Southfield, Michigan

Horton, Dale John
Stanley, New York

Howard, John Paul
Deerfield, Illinois

Inchauste, Ronald A.
La Paz, Bolivia

Jabbra, Roxanne Elizabeth
Mankato, Minnesota

Jehle, Mark Arthur
Alton, Illinois

Joseph, Andrew Sam
Zion, Illinois

Kelly, Richard Paul
Basking Ridge, New Jersey

Lawrence, William Joseph
Rock Island, Illinois

Leman, Samuel Earl Jr.
Bremen, Indiana

Lindroth, Alan Courtney
Waukegan, Illinois

McCoy, Timothy John
Hastings, Minnesota

Mosser, Douglas A.
Sandusky, Ohio

Muller, Michelle Jane
Sewickley, Pennsylvania

Murphy, James Alfred
Park Forest, Illinois

Nardi, Alfonso William
Springfield, Massachusetts

Niemiec, Leonard Roy Jr.
Northbrook, Illinois

Niewrzel, George Cass
Kansas City, Missouri

O'Neill, Patrick
Norwich, New York

Palmiter, Robert Jay Jr.
South Bend, Indiana

Paster, Michael James
Fair Haven, New Jersey

Pessemier, M. Blair
West Lafayette, Indiana

Pietrangeli, Romulo S.
Caracas, Venezuela

Policastro, Robert F.
New York, New York

Read, Frederick Kenneth
York, Pennsylvania

Rehman, Jamaluddin Adbul
Karachi, Pakistan

Rios, Esther Catalina
Rio Piedras, Puerto Rico

Robbins, Kirk J.
South Bend, Indiana

Ryan, William Patrick III
Colorado Springs, Colorado

Ryniak, Richard Alan
Southgate, Michigan

St. Jean, Joseph A. Jr.
South Bend, Indiana

Schneider, Susan Marie
St. Louis, Missouri

Schultz, Gregory Michael
Altoona, Pennsylvania

Serena, Martin Joseph II
Ottawa, Illinois

Sheehan, Francis Paul
Brownsburg, Indiana

Sinsky, Mark Francis
Milwaukee, Wisconsin

Snyder, Harold Jack Jr.
New Orleans, Louisiana

Stuermer, Cynthia
South Bend, Indiana

Turner, Alan Ernest
Youngstown, Ohio

Ward, Allan Leslie
South Bend, Indiana

Zannoni, Steven J.
Bratenahl, Ohio

Master of Science in Environic Design

el-Gohary, Osamah
Mohammed Noor
Riyadh, Saudi Arabia

Hoffheimer, Roger Steven
Cincinnati, Ohio

Kamio, Takefumi
Tokyo, Japan

Parent, Terrence P.
Chicago, Illinois

Patel, Lokesh F.
Notre Dame, Indiana

1977

Bachelor of Architecture

Amenta, Anthony James
Chadds Ford, Pennsylvania

Banas, Donald John
Glenview, Illinois

Bauman, Kathleen Melody
Fairview Park, Ohio

Boehm, Gary Joseph
Summerville, South Carolina

Buckley, Kevin John
Cohasset, Massachusetts

Bula, William John
West Lafayette, Indiana

Burger, John Michael Jr.
Las Vegas, Nevada

Caddigan, Robert Alan
Canton, Massachusetts

Canavan, Charles Patrick
Longmeadow, Massachusetts

Carrick, William Louis
Bridgeville, Pennsylvania

Causey, Jeffrey Bowen
Phoenix, Arizona

Chambers, Thomas Miles
La Grange, Illinois

Christ, Richard Alan
Carlyle, Illinois

Christien, Stephen Andrew
Chicago, Illinois

Connolly, Mark Richard
Mantoloking, New Jersey

Corcoran, Joseph Edward
Dallas, Texas

DiTolla, Robert John
Denver, Colorado

Doheny, Donald Aloysius Jr.
St. Louis, Missouri

Dolph, Joe Patrick
Lapaz, Indiana

Duffy, Patrick James
Pawtucket, Rhode Island

Eide, Jerome Fredrick
Fort Dodge, Iowa

Emma, Robert A.
Geneva, Illinois

Erkins, Melissa Hunt
Bliss, Idaho

Fahrenbach, Margaret Mary
Chicago, Illinois

Faron, Frank Martin
Indianhead Park, Illinois

Fransioli, Frank Fredrick
Gary, Indiana

Gallegos, Matthew Edward
Sanford, Colorado

Gertz, Stephen Paul
Plainview, New York

Green, Richard Owen
South Bend, Indiana

Hagan, Mary Elizabeth
Lexington, Kentucky

Harris, James William
Gaston, Indiana

Hazard, Michael Armand
Kew Gardens, New York

Hunter, Arlene Elizabeth
Mishawaka, Indiana

Johnson, Richard Francis
Xavier
Havertown, Pennsylvania

Katilas, Paul
Bound Brook, New Jersey

King, John Michael
Mountainside, New Jersey

Kortsch, William Joseph
Milwaukee, Wisconsin

LaVigne, William Robert
Rochester, New York

LeMay, Mark David
Fitchburg, Massachusetts

Lum, Wendell Wing On
Honolulu, Hawaii

Mack, David Joseph
Nashville, Tennessee

Mader, Daniel R.
Coldwater, Ohio

Margiotta, Arthur Francis
Morristown, New Jersey

Marqua, Charles E.
Stamford, Connecticut

Masterson, Thomas John
Ranchos Palos Verdes,
California

Mather, Deborah Kay
Bloomington, Indiana

McGrath, Mary Regina
Michigan City, Indiana

Meyer, Richard Allen
Crown Point, Indiana

Mulhern, Michael Gerrard
Crofton, Maryland

Nye, Christopher John
South Bend, Indiana

Peterman, Cherryl Juliet
Neshanic Station, New Jersey

Reale, Jay Kevin
Carmel, Indiana

Reich, Charles Edward
Baden, Pennsylvania

Rheingold, Michael Jacob
Albany, New York

Ryan, James L. Jr.
Pittsburgh, Pennsylvania

Scherry, David Charles
Avon Lake, Ohio

Schulze, Philip Roy
Fort Lauderdale, Florida

Sheehan, Thomas Francis Jr.
Bartlett, Illinois

Shiel, Barry Andrew
Chicago, Illinois

Stough, Patricia Marie
South Bend, Indiana

Sturm, William D.
Jasper, Indiana

Sweeney, Morgan John
Lynchburg, Virginia

Tuttle, James Thomas
Wolcott, Connecticut

Weber, Patricia Joy
Scarsdale, New York

Winchester, Joseph Scott
Dowagiac, Michigan

Yennerell, Robert Francis
Jeannette, Pennsylvania

1978

Bachelor of Architecture

Alonso, Francisco E.
Guaynabo, Puerto Rico

Antonucci, John Vincent
New Carlisle, Indiana

Becker, Lisa Louise
Erie, Pennsylvania

Bender, John David
Pinole, California

Blieszner, Edward J.
Pittsburgh, Pennsylvania

Boylan, Barbara Jeanne
Winchester, Massachusetts

Brady, Brian Patrick
Havertown, Pennsylvania

Budd, Mark Thomas
Fort Lauderdale, Florida

Burns, Joseph Gilmary
Columbus, Ohio

Carbone, Dominic G. Jr.
Pepper Pike, Ohio

Cipos, Mark Ernest
Stratford, Connecticut

Civitello, Robert Louis
Rochester, New York

Coleman, James Patrick
Latham, New York

Coleman, William Edward Jr.
Kailua, Hawaii

Corbin, Elizabeth Rose
Port Huron, Michigan

Courseault, LeRoy Martin
New Orleans, Louisiana

Cusick, Catherine Mary
Mt. Lebanon, Pennsylvania

Cyrus, Denis Neal
South Bend, Indiana

Davis, Terry Brent
Lebanon, Indiana

DeCrane, Peter John
Cleveland, Ohio

DeMarre, James Phillip
Fullerton, California

Demetrion, Thomas Gregory
Turners Falls, Massachusetts

Duncan, Kermit Edward
Greenville, Mississippi

Dzierla, Joseph Allen
South Bend, Indiana

Echavarria Uribe, Monica I.
Medellin, Colombia

Eddy, Joseph Stephen
Geneva, New York

Gaudreau, William Andrew
Lucien
Baltimore, Maryland

Gergel, Peter John
Chicago Heights, Illinois

Gibler, Susan Denise Hicks
Terre Haute, Indiana

Gorman, Michael Tennant
Sudbury, Massachusetts

Hanna, Joan Teresa
Rochester, New York

Hansen, Leo Cramer
Fort Lauderdale, Florida

Hayes, Daniel Francis Charles
Williamsport, Pennsylvania

Holmberg, James John
Columbus, Nebraska

Howard, Robert Stevens
Beaver Dam, Wisconsin

Inchauste, Mary Roetker
Lafayette, Indiana

Istvan, Joseph John
Rochester, New York

Koplin, Mark Alfred
Milwaukee, Wisconsin

Kovac, Daniel Peter
Westchester, Illinois

Lafferty, George Digby Jr.
Hollidaysburg, Pennsylvania

LaMonica, John Sebastian
Elkton, Maryland

Laughlin, Patrick Owen
Rockledge, Florida

L'Heureux, Stephen Michael
Bennington, Vermont

Madaras, George Michael
Palos Heights, Illinois

Madden, Paul Francis
Indianapolis, Indiana

Malewitz, William Reid
Jackson, Michigan

McAlpine, David William
Fort Lauderdale, Florida

Michel, Guy Elwood
Palos Heights, Illinois

Michel, William Charles
Palos Heights, Illinois

Mills, Robert Bradley
Tegucigalpa, Honduras

Munger, Hal Peter
Perrysburg, Ohio

Nolan, Michael Edward
Tulsa, Oklahoma

Novak, Nancy Joan
San Antonio, Texas

O'Brien, John Joseph
Birmingham, Michigan

O'Connell, John Patrick
Waynesburg, Pennsylvania

Otto, David William
Florissant, Missouri

Peckham, Gregory Robert
Richland Center, Wisconsin

Pichler, Daniel Joseph
Lansing, Michigan

Przybylowski, Thaddeus J. Jr.
Cheltenham, Pennsylvania

Przywara, Christopher
William
Runnemede, New Jersey

Pyn, Prudence Ann
Belle Harbor, New York

Rechtsteiner, Mark Joseph
Cincinnati, Ohio

Riley, Terence McGinnis
Crystal Lake, Illinois

Santello, Joseph Dominic
Lake Forest, Illinois

Sarnocinski, Edward John
Chester, Pennsylvania

Schneider, Charles Jacob
Buffalo, New York

Short, Jane Louise
Archbold, Ohio

Simonds, Reid E.
Chenango Forks, New York

Sosa Vallarino, Virgilio E.
Panama City, Panama

Stenz, William E.
Scottsdale, Arizona

Trevino Cantu, Abelardo
Los Angeles, California

Trinkaus, Clifford James
Neptune, New Jersey

Trzupek, Gregory Alan
Hammond, Indiana

Turnure, William Giles
Wilmington, Delaware

Waldock, Wade Charles
Olean, New York

Waldron, Martin Webb
Fort Wayne, Indiana

Walsh, Alix Ann
Port Washington, New York

Weithman, Gregory James
Plano, Texas

Wiley, Chris Eugene
Colorado Springs, Colorado

Master of Science in Environic Design

Grant, Philip Schuyler Jr.
Bernardsville, New Jersey

Mofti, Farooq Abbas
Mecca, Saudi Arabia

Pocius, Kestutis Kazimieras
East Chicago, Indiana

Sarb, Patrick Joseph
Dearborn, Michigan

Serruto, Thomas Mark
East Hartford, Connecticut

1979

Bachelor of Architecture

Alvarez, Salustiano
Guaynabo, Puerto Rico

Arzberger, Richard William
New Monmouth, New Jersey

Bailey, Thomas Anthony
Tonawanda, New York

Beery, Robert Vincent
Rochester, Indiana

Bruggeman, Mark Patrick
Middletown, Ohio

Bula, Joseph Matthias
West Lafayette, Indiana

Cahill, Kevin John
Summit, New Jersey

Chandler, James Thomas
Fort Wayne, Indiana

Clarke, Robert Edward
Annapolis, Maryland

Cooke, Daniel Allan
La Grange, Illinois

Coyle, James Butler III
East Greenwich,
Rhode Island

De Bruyne, Dale Thomas
Mishawaka, Indiana

Destino, David Mark
Niagara Falls, New York

Dever, Thomas James
Thornton, Pennsylvania

Dolinar, Joseph Patrick
Buffalo, New York

Dumont, Francis Xavier
Cherry Hill, New Jersey

Durocher, Charles Bernard
East Hartford, Connecticut

Erickson, Peter H.
River Forest, Illinois

Escoffery, Loraine Blanche
Chappaqua, New York

Falash, Mike Allan
Twin Falls, Idaho

Fordonski, Steven
Matteson, Illinois

French, Kathryn C.
Hartford, Connecticut

Fritsch, James A.
Batesville, Indiana

Grant, Philip Schuyler Jr.
Bernardsville, New Jersey

Hatem, Paul Joseph Anthony
Methuen, Massachusetts

Hellinghausen, Donald
Michael
Midland, Texas

Hiegel, Robert Stephen
North Little Rock, Arkansas

Hinken, Michael Van Dyce Jr.
Rockford, Illinois

Iandolo, Stephen Sheridan
Rockville, Maryland

Iwaszkiewicz, John Richard
Chicago, Illinois

Jurgielewicz, Mark Stephen
McLean, Virginia

Kiel, David Wilson
San Antonio, Texas

Krukiel, Joseph Mark
Tulsa, Oklahoma

Lessard, Raymond Eugene
Woonsocket, Rhode Island

Long, Douglas Gregory
Attica, Indiana

Loughery, Robert Joseph
Indianapolis, Indiana

Mallardi, Michael B.
Muskegon, Michigan

Manfredi, David Peter
South Glastonbury, Indiana

Masano, Thomas Frank
Reading, Pennsylvania

McElroy, James Francis
Trumbull, Connecticut

McGah, Katherine Marie
Elmhurst, Illinois

McWalters, Thomas J.
Berkeley, California

Miller, Henry Hazard
Devon, Pennsylvania

Moynahan, John Patrick
Evanston, Illinois

Murphy, Martin Joseph
Osceola, Indiana

Murray, Brian John
Libertyville, Illinois

Murray, F. Jeffrey
Penn Hills, Pennsylvania

Nieman, Robert Lee
Hinsdale, Illinois

Nolan, John Edward Jr.
Pittsburgh, Pennsylvania

Nook, Patrick William
South Haven, Michigan

Nugent, Richard Kevin
Babylon, New York

O'Brien, Denis Francis O'Flynn
Wilmington, Delaware

Ogburn, William Douglas
Louisville, Kentucky

Pearse, John Patrick
Dix Hills, New York

Pladna, Philip Raymond
Catonsville, Maryland

Pozzi, Scott Michael
San Bruno, California

Pruessner, Sandra Kay
Richmond, Indiana

Ryan, Kathleen Margaret
Elmhurst, Illinois

Rydle, John Arthur
Canonsburg, Pennsylvania

Sterner, James Gerard
Chicago, Illinois

Streit, Michael Ralph
Aurora, Illinois

Strollo, Gregg James
Canfield, Ohio

Swenton, Jeffrey John
Bristol, Connecticut

Swintal, James Henry
South Bend, Indiana

Taylor, Paul Lawrence Jr.
Wappingers Falls, New York

Trier, Mark Edward
Louisville, Kentucky

Trovato, Joseph Anthony
Rosedale, New York

Vitullo, Richard J.
Wilmette, Illinois

Wolfe, Donald Fanning Jr.
Fair Lawn, New Jersey

Zimmerman, Mark Edward
Wauwatosa, Wisconsin

1980

Bachelor of Architecture

Angelo, Russell John
Vineland, New Jersey

Bickler, Patrick Charles
Salem, Oregon

Bogan, John Joseph IV
Brielle, New Jersey

Bradford, Daniel Paul
Hull, Massachusetts

Campbell, Hugh J.
Brooklyn, New York

Carrera, Clara Maria
San Juan, Puerto Rico

Ceci, Joseph Louis
Milwaukee, Wisconsin

Cheatle, Brian Thomas
Freehold, New Jersey

Clemons, David Michael
Port Clinton, Ohio

Collins, Winston Francis
Westport, Connecticut

Cooper, Curtis Allyn
Hauppauge, New York

Costello, Kevin Michael
Monroe, Michigan

Crisafi, Anthony William
Bay Village, Ohio

Davidson, Peter Alcantara
Charlotte, North Carolina

De Celles, Paul Craig
South Bend, Indiana

DiBlasi, Michael Paul
North Kingstown,
Rhode Island

Donovan, Brian Shannon
Cincinnati, Ohio

Dyball, Kevin
Park Ridge, Illinois

Engelland, Bradford Joseph
Elyria, Ohio

Fallon, Kevin John
Stamford, Connecticut

Feeney, James William
Ivesdale, Illinois

Finn, Terrence Michael
St. Louis, Missouri

Follas, Theodore Robert
Grandview, Missouri

Fromholt, Thomas Joseph
Dayton, Ohio

Fujawa, Robert Edward
South Bend, Indiana

Gauvreau, Edmond George
Enfield, Connecticut

Grzesiak, Lynne E.
Sauqvoit, New York

Hart, Kevin David
Birmingham, Michigan

Herbert, William Karl
Auburn, New York

Hoerauf, Geralyn Clare
Birmingham, Michigan

Huderwitz, Francis Charles Jr.
Belford, New Jersey

Johantgen, Peter Francis
Brockport, New York

Kapczuk, Paul Jr.
Orange Village, Ohio

Kerchaert, Kevin J.
Denver, Colombia

Kwasnowski, James Peter
Kingston, New York

Lacey, Michael Kevin
Catonsville, Maryland

Landolt, Allan Joseph
Virginia, Illinois

Lisch, Russell John
Belleville, Illinois

Lung, Kyle Patrick
Kailua, Hawaii

Mayberry, Wade Hawks
Goshen, Indiana

McCabe, Thomas Corbin
Dover, Delaware

Meaney, Thomas Gerard
Santa Barbara, California

Meehan, Judith Anne
Gladwyne, Pennsylvania

Mercadante, Michael Thomas
Wethersfield, Connecticut

Metzler, Gary Paul
Grand Rapids, Michigan

Mongold, Neal Joseph
Creve Coeur, Missouri

Munana, Suzanne Marie
Madrid, Spain

Narducci, Domenic A. III
Naugatuck, Connecticut

Natale, Michael Andrew
North Versailles,
Pennsylvania

Nilles, Steven Michael
Fargo, North Dakota

O'Connell, Kathleen
Plymouth, Michigan

O'Neill, George Edward
Lowell, Massachusetts

O'Reilly, Kevin Matthew
South Bend, Indiana

Padro, Janice Lee
Rio Piedras, Puerto Rico

Pouler, Patrick John
Trevor, Wisconsin

Quinn, Gregory Philip
Olympia Fields, Illinois

Richert, James Joseph
Winamac, Indiana

Richmond, Kenneth Calvin
Sparta, Michigan

Schleck, Raymond Mathias II
Prospect, Kentucky

Stankard, Mark Raymond
Akron, Ohio

Steedle, James Paul
Pittsburgh, Pennsylvania

Tassinari, Mark Joseph
West Springfield,
Massachusetts

Teves, Richard Earl
South Bend, Indiana

Tierney, Karen Elizabeth
Pittsfield, Massachusetts

Walters, Julia Virginia
Springfield, Illinois

Wegener, Robert David
Alton, Illinois

Figure 83. **Outside the Forum, Rome, 1984.**

Figure 86. **Albergo Lunetta, 1997.**

Figure 84. **Ostia Antica, 1996.**

Figure 87. **Temple of Hera, Sicily, 1978.**

Figure 85. **At Hadrian's Villa, 1996.**

Figure 88. **Their Royal Highnesses, 1956.**

Figure 89. **Rock-a-bye Babies, 1958.**

Figure 90. **The Metallic Look, 1957.**

Figure 91. **Dante's Inferno, Rome, 1973.**

Figure 92. **"Pseudo" Theme, 1958.**

Figure 93. **In a Blue Mood, Rome, 1996.**

Figure 94. Wielding t-squares in the studio, 1950.

Figure 95. At the drafting table, 1957.

Figure 96. On the construction site, Chicago 1980.

Figure 97. An award-winning design, 1961.

Figure 98. **The Graduate Class of 1997.**

Figure 99. **In the fourth-year studio, 1999.**

Figure 100. **Commencement Day, 1998.**

1981

Bachelor of Architecture

Ainge, Gary Michael
Springfield, Ohio

Behles, Joseph John
Glenview, Illinois

Berenato, Daniel Andrew
Ventnor, New Jersey

Box, William Everett
South Bend, Indiana

Breiner, David Michael
Jersey City, New Jersey

Brown, William Michael
Munster, Indiana

Brunner, Patrick Mason
Fort Wayne, Indiana

Cabrera, Guillermo E.
San Juan, Puerto Rico

Caines, Robert Earle Jr.
Rochester, New York

Carrero, Carlos Alberto
San German, Puerto Rico

Chalifoux, Matthew Stuart
Pennington, New Jersey

Colaluca, James Richard
New Castle, Pennsylvania

Cotten, Lisa Ann
Orange Park, Florida

Cullum, Thomas D.
Evansville, Indiana

De Sapio, Martin Anthony
Baptistown, New Jersey

Debelius, Timothy John
Alexandria, Virginia

Demmerle, Mark A.
New Canaan, Connecticut

Dickinson, Douglas Frank
Ticonderoga, New York

Doherty, Michael Thomas
South Bend, Indiana

Dreyer, Allan Bernard
Greenwood, Indiana

Fitzgerald, Richard William
Indianapolis, Indiana

Franklin, Oliver Hollis
Chicago, Illinois

Gall, Glenn Saint Aubin
Beverly, Massachusetts

Garofalo, Douglas Anthony
Clifton Park, New York

Gazzerro, Michael John
Dayton, Ohio

Goliber, Jeffry Michael
Painted Post, New York

Gomez, Maria Cristina
Lake Forest, Illinois

Haradem, Denise
Avon, Ohio

Hedge, William Nelson Jr.
South Bend, Indiana

Jehring, John Randall
Naples, Florida

Kaiser, Richard Joseph
Monticello, New York

Kane, Kevin John
Grand Ledge, Michigan

Kelly, Brian Paul
Denville, New Jersey

Kelsch, Paul Joseph
Fairfield, Connecticut

Kennedy, Christopher Peter
Laurel, Maryland

Kenrick, Thomas James
Warren, Michigan

Kitchen, Mark Joseph
South Charleston, Ohio

Kudlacz, Stanley Adam Jr.
La Grange, Illinois

Lapeyre, Maria Ann
New Orleans, Louisiana

LaVigne, Joseph Charles
Rochester, New York

Lee, Michael Anthony
St. Patrick
Kingston, Jamaica

Leone, Donald Laurence Jr.
Riverside, Illinois

Lyon, Thomas Francis
South Bend, Indiana

MacDonald, Michael Anthony
Medfield, Massachusetts

Mazza, Anthony John
Wilmington, Delaware

McInerny, Anne Marie
South Bend, Indiana

Miller, Mark Douglas
Bettendorf, Iowa

Morris, S. Allan
Grand Prairie, Texas

Noone, Peter John
Glens Falls, New York

Nucciarone, Joseph George
Huntington Beach, California

O'Keefe, Erin Marie
Greenlawn, New York

O'Meara, Kathleen M.
South Bend, Indiana

O'Neill, James William Jr.
Dallas, Texas

Oprisch, Mark Daniel
Fairfield, Connecticut

Orban, Donald Allen
Fort Wayne, Indiana

Ortale, Victor Fusia
Nashville, Tennessee

Ouellette, Edward Guy
Lexington, Kentucky

Pasyk, Rodney Michael
Hammond, Indiana

Power, Theresa Mary
Duluth, Minnesota

Reed, Jessie Ellen
Dover Plains, New York

Robertson, Daniel L.
Sunrise, Florida

Rodgers, Edward Alfred
Gaithersburg, Maryland

Rooney, John Bryan
Convent Station, New Jersey

Ryan, Mary Michael
Janesville, Wisconsin

Sagardia, Jose Miguel
San Juan, Puerto Rico

Savory, Thomas Wesley
Cheyenne, Wyoming

Schliesmann, Jeffry Joseph
Racine, Wisconsin

Schoenherr, David Francis
Rochester, New York

Sherer, Thomas Edward Jr.
West Hartford, Connecticut

Siegrist, Peter Joseph
Appleton, Wisconsin

Siemer, Kathleen Margaret
Rockford, Illinois

Smyth, Brian Patrick Dillon
Bethesda, Maryland

Swindler, Robert Charles
Fort Wayne, Indiana

Taylor, Brendan Bartholomew
Cumberland, Maryland

Teske, Eric Albert
Cincinnati, Ohio

Theisen, Charles Edward
Mishawaka, Indiana

Vallorz, Albert Louis
Chatham, Illinois

Weigel, Robert Steven
Danielson, Connecticut

Zucker, Gwenneth Tina
Wappingers Falls, New York

1982

Bachelor of Architecture

Abrego, Leopoldo Antonio
San Salvador, El Salvador

Bingham, Kenneth William
Cranford, New Jersey

Brown, Steven Alan
Chesterfield, Missouri

Carr, Thomas Vincent
Washington, D.C.

Carrig, Christopher Charles
Sterling, Illinois

Craig, Patricia Ann
South Bend, Indiana

Dube, Vincent Emile John
Pepperell, Massachusetts

Figg, Dennis Alan
Plymouth, Indiana

Fishman, Mary Christine
Chicago, Illinois

Flood, Timothy Patrick
Janesville, Wisconsin

Flores, Robert
El Paso, Texas

Gamez, Evelyn Celeste
San Antonio, Texas

Gates, Paul Ritter
Louisville, Kentucky

Goleski, Michael P.
Tulsa, Oklahoma

Helle, Robert H.
River Forest, Illinois

Hinojosa, Gustavo Noel
San Antonio, Texas

Ineson, John Robert
Southbury, Connecticut

Janer, Javier Manuel
San Juan, Puerto Rico

Jeselnick, Paul Rene
St. Mary's, Pennsylvania

Joiner, Jocelyn Griselda
Huntsville, Alabama

Kenney, Linda Susan
Springfield, Illinois

Kierzkowski, Michael
Anthony
Lancaster, Pennsylvania

Kowalski, Michelle Andrea
Southampton, Pennsylvania

Lacey, Ronald Albert Jr.
Elkhart, Indiana

Loustau, Jeffrey Justin
San Francisco, California

Marsh, Douglas K.
South Bend, Indiana

McDermott, John Dennis
Cambridge, Massachusetts

McLean, David J.
Bethel Park, Pennsylvania

McNichols, Brian Joseph
Milton, Wisconsin

McShane, Kevin James
Pittsburgh, Pennsylvania

Molina, Luis Eugenio
Santiago, Chile

Molinelli, Michael Joseph
Briarcliff Manor, New York

Monardo, Paul Joseph
Pittsburgh, Pennsylvania

Moore, Mitchell Walter
Phoenix, Arizona

Moriarity, Daniel Thomas
Cambridge, Illinois

Murray, Elizabeth Hope
Devon, Pennsylvania

Nelson, Jane Ann
Scobey, Montana

Nyberg, Teresa Ann
Oakdale, Massachusetts

O'Brien, Matthew Gerald
St. Paul, Minnesota

Penate, Antonio Francisco
San Juan, Puerto Rico

Reynolds, John Matthew
Lowell, Indiana

Riese, Stephen Robert
Leavenworth, Kansas

Ritger, Robert Charles
Mendham, New Jersey

Role, Richard Branton
Addison, Illinois

Schunk, Diane Angela
Williamsville, New York

Swindler, Ellen Schmeltz
Kansas City, Kansas

Tewey, Brian Patrick
Venice, Florida

Thiel, Barbara Vogel
Hudson, Ohio

Tizio, Gregory Thomas
Saddle Brook, New Jersey

Toro, Guy Christopher
Stone Mountain, Georgia

Walker, Carmetta La Joyce
Fort Wayne, Indiana

Walker, Robert Philip
Bristol, Indiana

Welch, Richard John
Belmont, Massachusetts

Wise, Julie Virginia
Fort Collins, Colorado

1983

Bachelor of Architecture

Bell, Matthew James
McMurray, Pennsylvania

Boyle, Timothy William
Trumbull, Connecticut

Burns, Anne Marie
Columbus, Ohio

Carbery, Stephen Raymond
Lockport, Illinois

Carroll, Edward Andrew
Dayton, New Jersey

Cashman, Stephen John
Holmes Beach, Florida

Cherney, Diane M.
Newark, Delaware

Costello, Leslie Ann
La Jolla, California

Dobrowski, Marie M.
Shaker Heights, Ohio

Dowd, John Dennis
Springfield, Massachusetts

DuConge, John Joseph
New Orleans, Louisiana

Duffey, James Edward
Scituate, Massachusetts

Dunn, Terrence Patrick James
Cleveland, Ohio

Edmonds, Matthew Eugene
Garden Grove, California

Frederickson, Frederick Scott
Medford, New Jersey

Goodill, Robert Stephen
Erie, Pennsylvania

Grich, Robert Mason
Burke, Virginia

Hardy, Michael Joseph
Warwick, Rhode Island

Hayes, Kevin Albert
Pittsburgh, Pennsylvania

Heisler, Paul C.
Houston, Texas

Heppard, Wesley Philip
Peoria, Illinois

Hinchman, Mark Alan
Charlotte, North Carolina

Hinders, Kevin John
Kettering, Ohio

Hofman, Thomas Christopher
South Bend, Indiana

Hudson, Jane Ann
Mishawaka, Indiana

Hussey, Daniel Martin
Goshen, Indiana

Jacob, Paul Christian
Fairfield, Connecticut

Jeffries, Gregory
Chicago, Illinois

Jehle, Laura M.
Buffalo, New York

Kizer, David L.
La Paz, Indiana

Klucka, Charles Vincent
Birmingham, Michigan

Kot, Gregory Peter
Fairfax, Virginia

Leblang, Mark Wayne
Mishawaka, Indiana

Maddalena, Benjamin Dean
Ann Arbor, Michigan

Marrero, Keith Joseph
New Orleans, Louisiana

Mayernik, David Thomas
Allentown, Pennsylvania

Meyer, Michael David
Lawrenceberg, Indiana

Morgan, Roger Philip
Thienville, Wisconsin

Mortensen, Paul Robert
Tacoma, Washington

Murphy, Shanne Miller
Norfolk, Virginia

Murray, Joseph A.
Columbus, Ohio

Norman, Jeffrey Alan
Lebanon, Pennsylvania

Perry, Jeff George
Sudbury, Canada

Placco, Christopher Oscar
Pawtucket, Rhode Island

Rajkovich, Thomas Norman
Griffith, Indiana

Roach, Linda Gail
Tallahassee, Florida

Seleme, Margaret Doris
La Paz, Bolivia

Shanley, Michael Kerry
South Bend, Indiana

Shannon, Daniel Patrick
Louisville, Kentucky

Sidabras, Dalia Irena
Munster, Indiana

Spatz, Amy Louise
Naperville, Illinois

Stanton, John Patrick Jr.
Lemont, Illinois

Tang, Roland Tsai-Yee
Hong Kong

VanAuken, Jacqueline Ann
Shaker Heights, Ohio

VanPatten, Victoria Beth
South Bend, Indiana

Westbrook, Timothy Jon
Livonia, New York

Zahn, Gregory Gerard
Appleton, Wisconsin

1984

Bachelor of Architecture

Anhut, Thomas John
Ypsilanti, Michigan

Arvin, Scott Anthony
Loogootee, Indiana

Bastian, John Edward
South Bend, Indiana

Beckner, Nancy Ann
East Stroudsburg,
Pennsylvania

Berndt, Gregory Vincent
South Bend, Indiana

Blakey, Matthew Menard
James
South Bend, Indiana

Brehm, Gregory John
Palatine, Illinois

Casacio, Denise Joy
Elkin Park, Pennsylvania

Clements, John Charles
Monterrey, Mexico

Corbett, Catherine Patterson
South Bend, Indiana

Crumlish, Brendan Daniel
Palmer
South Bend, Indiana

Doane, David B.
Norfolk, Nebraska

Feehery, John Michael
Springfield, Pennsylvania

Froehlke, Paul R.
Barrington, Illinois

Gabaldon, Dominic Gerard
Belen, New Mexico

Garcia Muchacho, Maria
Eugenia
Maracaibo, Venezuela

Gaylord, Kenneth James
Libertyville, Illinois

Guljas, Andrew Alan
Commiskey, Indiana

Haemmerle, Steven James
Naperville, Illinois

Horky, John George
Wauwatosa, Wisconsin

Hovancik, Charles Michael III
Chenango Forks, New York

Hsiang-chung, Cheng
Taipei, Taiwan

Johnson, Steven James
McMurray, Pennsylvania

Kehler, Elvira Regina
South Bend, Indiana

Klamon, Charles Andrew
St. Louis, Missouri

Kronstein, Veronika
South Bend, Indiana

Lamb, Daniel James
Flint, Michigan

Liese, William Joseph
Dallas, Texas

Lopez, Michael Martin
East Chicago, Indiana

Lopez-Aguilar, Javier
Puebla, Mexico

Lucero, John Anthony
Espanola, New Mexico

Luetkehans, Mark Steven
Wheaton, Illinois

Masini, Jon B.
St. Joseph, Michigan

Matthews, Gretchen Lee
Barrington, Rhode Island

McCabe, Kevin Michael
Inverness, Illinois

McManus, Martin Patrick
South Bend, Indiana

Meadows, David Glen
Paoli, Indiana

Noonan, Timothy Dolan
St. Louis, Missouri

Nyers, Richard Alex
South Bend, Indiana

O'Brien, Cheryl A.
Canton, Ohio

O'Connell, Joanne Colmcille
Monterey, Massachusetts

Owens, Joyce Ellen
Merrillville, Indiana

Pancoe, Sandra Marie
Leechburg, Pennsylvania

Peters, Richard J.
Gurnee, Illinois

Rectenwald, Daniel James
Duluth, Minnesota

Rickling, Brian Stephen
San Diego, California

Schellinger, James Armand
South Bend, Indiana

Severino, Alexander Henry
La Grange, Illinois

Skahan, Edward F.
St. Cloud, Minnesota

Smith, Heather Lynne
Shaker Heights, Ohio

Soranno, Joan Marie
St. Paul, Minnesota

Stone, Randall Craig
Tulsa, Oklahoma

Talty, Jon P.
Western Springs, Illinois

Toohey, Jeffrey Gerald
Omaha, Nebraska

1985

Bachelor of Architecture

Berger, Scott Edward
Hackettstown, New Jersey

Burch, Dennis Gerard
Loogootee, Indiana

Clifford, William Barnett
Greeley, Colorado

Cormane, Curtis Frank
Hong Kong

Curtin, James Michael
Austin, Texas

DeGraw, Thomas Jeffrey
Bellvale, New York

Derwent, Margaret Mary
South Bend, Indiana

Dudney, James Christopher
Chambersburg, Pennsylvania

Eagles, Tim Stocker
Battle Creek, Michigan

Eyler, Therese Patricia
San Marino, California

Fisher, Mark Rolland
Coloma, Michigan

Gaudreau, David Gerard
Baltimore, Maryland

Gauthier, Douglas J.
Flint, Michigan

Haynes, William Jude
Indianapolis, Indiana

Henderson, Ronald Eric
Salem, Indiana

Isley, Jeffrey Scott
Tulsa, Oklahoma

Janicki, John Peter
Sedro Woolley, Washington

Janovsky, Eric Ronald
Arlington, Texas

Jett, Cynthia Louise
Bethel Park, Pennsylvania

Keleher, Daniel Joseph Jr.
Bartlesville, Oklahoma

Koplas, John Richard
Lockport, New York

La Chance, Matthew Gerard
Aurora, Illinois

Mariani, Theodore Mark
Washington, D.C.

McGrath, Joseph Ammon
Warrington, Pennsylvania

Miller, Jeffrey David
Birmingham, Alabama

Nauta, Debra Ann
Andover, New Jersey

Pellissier, Joseph Brian
Ware, Massachusetts

Peters, Glenford Rudolph
Chicago, Illinois

Pitchford, Joseph Francis
Norfolk, Virginia

Pratt, Susan Elizabeth
Fair Oaks, California

Rebholz, Steven Vincent
Rochester, New York

Sassano, David John
South Bend, Indiana

Spencer, Barry Steven
Detroit, Michigan

Sponseller, Robert Michael
Ann Arbor, Michigan

Tripeny, Patrick John
Casper, Wyoming

Turner, Bruce Durant
Medford, New Jersey

Vento, Arthur John
Fort Lauderdale, Florida

Vician, Kevin Michael
Crown Point, Indiana

Wehner, Robert Lawrence
Danville, California

Willenbrink, Edward Lawrence
Louisville, Kentucky

Wilson, David Scott
Los Angeles, California

Wolf, Bonnie Jean
Waukesha, Wisconsin

1986

Bachelor of Architecture

Bailey, Deloris Yvonne
Richmond, Virginia

Baldo, Luis Felipe
Notre Dame, Indiana

Batistich, Simon Nicholas
Lemont, Illinois

Carl, Edward Tim
Elkhart, Indiana

Carr, Richard Charles II
Topsfield, Massachusetts

Comas, Noris Teresa
Rio Piedras, Puerto Rico

Daniels, Darryl Harmon
Berkeley, California

Deleone, Paul Anthony
Dana Point, California

DiGiorno, Vincent John
Boca Raton, Florida

Duchynski, Cheryl Ann
Reading, Pennsylvania

Funai, Craig Yasu
Fair Lawn, New Jersey

Gaskin, Arthur Jude
Norfolk, Virginia

Gavagan, Edward Martin
Cheyenne, Wyoming

Griffin, Toni Lynn
Chicago, Illinois

Hamilton, Michael Thomas
Minooka, Illinois

Jackson, Elaine Patricia
Johnstown, Pennsylvania

Jasper, Michael Scott
Davenport, Iowa

Kane, Mary Margaret
Grand Ledge, Michigan

Keating, Daniel Philip
Fort Devens, Massachusetts

Leach, Dennis Michael
Pennsauken, New Jersey

Maglietta, Mary Augusta
Freeport, Illinois

Marr, Alfredo Oscar
Twenty-nine Palms,
California

Masters, Ronald Joseph II
Atlantic Beach, Florida

McCauley, Emil Joseph
Libertyville, Illinois

Miles, David Joseph
South Bend, Indiana

Mollet, Bradley David
Burbank, South Dakota

Munro, Christopher Lukas
Augusta, Maine

Murray, Douglas Patrick
East Hampton, Connecticut

Muth, Gregory Paul
Oklahoma City, Oklahoma

Nakao, Kerry T.
Torrance, California

O'Brien, Sean Patrick
Phillipsburg, New Jersey

Olarte, Andres
Medellin, Colombia

Oppenborn, Robert Gustav
Oak Park, Illinois

O'Toole, Mary Brigid
Chicago, Illinois

Poynton, Michael James
Doylestown, Pennsylvania

Ramey, Martha Adelia Ellis
Midland, Texas

Schmid, Paul Edward
Mauldin, South Carolina

Smith, Jeffrey Mark
Marietta, Georgia

Smith, Stephen Michael
South Bend, Indiana

Timm, Mary Elizabeth
Michigan City, Indiana

VanArsdale, Adele Simone
Waterloo, Iowa

Wasilak, Ronald James
Pittsburgh, Pennsylvania

Weidmann, Kurt James
Loudonville, New York

Wilson, William Charles
Buenos Aires, Argentina

Wowkowych, Peter Dmytro
Rochester, New York

Zimmerman, Kurt Vincent
Hartland, Wisconsin

1987

Bachelor of Architecture

Arnold, Timothy Leon
Long Beach, California

Bernal, Maria Francisca
Guaynabo, Puerto Rico

Browne, Paul William
Stamford, Connecticut

Casolo, Michael A. P.
Norwalk, Connecticut

Clements, Mahlon
Christopher
Canton, New York

Coghlan, Philip Andrew
Fredericton, Canada

Cohoon, Robert Gerald
Naperville, Illinois

Cooper, Gary Rogers
Brooklyn, New York

Dixon, Kerry Anne
Philo, Illinois

Fitzgerald, Michael Green
Lake Forest, Illinois

Garcia, Margarita Josefina
Rio Piedras, Puerto Rico

Gester, David John
Palos Hills, Illinois

Gomez, Ginette
Okemos, Michigan

Graham, Mary Helen
Pacific Palisades, California

Hanahan, Michael Joseph
Birmingham, Michigan

Hand, Sarah Elizabeth
Sherborn, Massachusetts

Hayden, Patrick Joseph
Bogota, New Jersey

Herrmann, Brian Scott
Fountain City, Indiana

Irving, Mark Patrick
Fullerton, California

Jakubik, Robert Joseph
Barrington, Illinois

Johnson, Audrey J.
South Bend, Indiana

Kaahaaina, David Bismarck
Noheaikawekiu Jr.
Honolulu, Hawaii

Kane, James Thomas
Olyphant, Pennsylvania

Kapitan, Joseph Michael
Broadview Heights, Ohio

Kennedy, John Charles
Dallas, Texas

Kloc, Daniel Charles
South Bend, Indiana

Kraft, John Leonard
Oak Park, Illinois

Kramer, Paul Allan
Chagrin Falls, Ohio

McDonough, Peggy Ann
Salt Lake City, Utah

Miggins, Brendan Thomas
Trumbull, Connecticut

Murphy, Timothy John
Eastchester, New York

Niemeyer, Lucian Lenzner
Aston, Pennsylvania

Rich, Scott Anthony
  Bolton, Connecticut
Salazar, Mauricio
  Kingwood, Texas
Shreve, John Patrick
  Stockton, California
Valade, Jay Lawrence Jr.
  Trumbull, Connecticut
Walter, Tara Michele
  Eastchester, New York
Wiggins, Carl Edgar Jr.
  East Orange, New Jersey
Wisneski, Michael Daniel
  Colorado Springs, Colorado
Zande, Michelle Ann
  Worthington, Ohio

Master of Architecture

Callahan, Kevin Lee
  Indianapolis, Indiana
Fitzgerald, Edward Lisle
  Albuquerque, New Mexico
Kil, Gregory A.
  South Bend, Indiana

1988

Bachelor of Architecture

Buehler, Shelane Ann
  Ridgway, Pennsylvania
Burgoyne, Michael Scott
  Burnsville, Minnesota
Choi, Charles
  Seoul, Korea
Conroy, Brian Francis
  Allen Park, Michigan
Diaz, Rodrigo
  Guatemala City, Guatemala
Esteve, Jose Eduardo
  Dallas, Texas
Galicia, Dominic Quimbo
  Notre Dame, Indiana
Georgiou, Maria George
  Nicosia, Cyprus
Goblirsch, James Albert
  Arlington, Minnesota
Grantham, Thomas David
  Madison, Wisconsin
Harrington, Catherine Ann
  Northboro, Massachusetts
Karl, Edward Joseph
  Pittsburgh, Pennsylvania
Kelty, Matthew Gerard
  Kendallville, Indiana
Kohlhaas, Kimberly Ruth
  Austin, Texas
Kromkowski, Stephen Paul
  Baltimore, Maryland
Lamb, Thomas Everett
  Tampa, Florida
Llano, Eduardo
  Coral Gables, Florida
Loretto, Virgil Nelson
  Naschitti, New Mexico

Lusser, Rene Joseph
  Ballwin, Missouri
McCabe, John Joseph Jr.
  Asharoken, New York
McGowan, James Carlton
  Mercer Island, Washington
Milana, Paul Russell
  Tampa, Florida
Mould, Patricia Louise
  Columbus, Ohio
Napier, Suzanne
  Atlanta, Georgia
Naughton, Joseph A. III
  Indianapolis, Indiana
Otto, Jeffrey Philip
  St. Louis, Missouri
Russell, Jeffrey John
  Lynn Haven, Florida
Sherali, Hafiz-Ur-Rehman
  Karachi, Pakistan
Stadler, Deborah Marie
  Lexington, Kentucky
Tadych, Christopher Allen
  Berea, Ohio
Torrens D'Brasis, Rafael Angel
  Rio Piedras, Puerto Rico
Twohy, Peter Richard
  Aberdeen, New Jersey
Ventura, Marc Edwin
  Kapaa, Hawaii
Wagner, Barbara Ann
  Richland, Michigan
Woehl, Kristin Marie
  Alamo, California

Master of Architecture

Placco, Christopher Oscar
  Providence, Rhode Island

1989

Bachelor of Architecture

Anderson, Ann Louise
  Montclair, New Jersey
Brehm, Matthew Thomas
  Palatine, Illinois
Carreira, Rafael Suarez
  Northbrook, Illinois
Demitroff, Ann Elizabeth
  Kingston, Rhode Island
Evans, Christian Gerard
  Lake Oswego, Oregon
Hill, David Richard
  South Bend, Indiana
Keys, Reynauldt Ulysses
  Chicago, Illinois
Kirk, John Thomas
  St. Paul, Minnesota
Lanciault, Eric Thomas
  Sidney, New York
Leavell, Patrick Robin
  Elwood, Indiana
Manley, Thomas Roger II
  Merritt Island, Florida

McGuire, Michael Patrick
  Easton, Connecticut
Morita, Steven Shigeo
  Honolulu, Hawaii
Mulhall, Kevin John
  Berwyn, Pennsylvania
Murphy, Patrick Leo
  Gardner, Massachusetts
Patino, John Christopher
  Easton, Pennsylvania
Pedersen, Niels Frederik
  Fort Worth, Texas
Reno, Joye Kimberly
  Niagara on Lake, Canada
Roeder, Douglas Noel
  Niles, Michigan
Skendzel, Richard Adam
  Traverse City, Michigan
Tedesco, John Patrick
  Glens Falls, New York
VanderLaan, John Richard
  Bay Village, Ohio
Wehner, James Lee
  Salix, Pennsylvania
Weidmann, Brian David
  Loudonville, New York

Master of Architecture

Angelini, Bradford Lee
  Newport, Rhode Island
Angelini, Theresa Luthman
  Columbus, Ohio
Goswami, Bulbul Biswas
  Calcutta, India
Li, Wei
  Beijing, China
Santi-Canache, Claudio A.
  Caracas, Venezuela

1990

Bachelor of Architecture

Adams, John Patrick
  New Philadelphia, Ohio
Bajandas, Roberto Joseph
  Louisville, Kentucky
Bezilla, Brian Eugene
  Exeter, New Hampshire
Bohan, Peter Ducey
  Shaker Heights, Ohio
Brangle, Timothy Sean
  St. Louis, Missouri
Brennan, Patrick Anthony
  Aberdeen, Washington
Chura, Joseph E.
  Cleveland, Ohio
Dever, Patricia Ann
  Bethel, Connecticut
Edmonds, Bradley Frayser
  Oklahoma City, Oklahoma
Endler, Patrick John
  Wilkes-Barre, Pennsylvania
Fehlner, Anne Marie
  South Bend, Indiana

Galvin, Amy Karen
  Munster, Indiana
Garrett, Sean Michael
  Troy, Michigan
Gatti, Michael Maurice
  Woodcliff Lake, New Jersey
Gonzalez, Lorena
  Corpus Christi, Texas
Gonzalez, Monica
  Corpus Christi, Texas
Grahek, Matthew John
  Fairlawn, Ohio
Hatcher, Nolanda James
  Fairfield, Alabama
Hines, F. Russell
  Wayland, Massachusetts
Horton, Bernadette Marie
  Flossmoor, Illinois
Indeglia, Paul Anthony
  Narragansett, Rhode Island
Kelly, Paul Joseph
  Omaha, Nebraska
Krueger, Karl Allen
  Vail, Colorado
Leighton, Louise
  Mishawaka, Indiana
Lynch, Patrick Dennis
  Seattle, Washington
Mayer, Edward Michael
  Mountainside, New Jersey
McCraw, William Gary
  Arlington, Texas
McRoberts, Duncan
McCallum
  Eugene, Oregon
Munger, David James
  Perrysburg, Ohio
New, Steven
  South Bend, Indiana
Ng, Kai Chung
  Hong Kong
O'Halloran, Margaret Ann
  La Grange, Illinois
O'Neil, Mary Bridget
  Port Byron, New York
Onorato, Martin Alexander
  Geneva, New York
Pinto, Jose Antonio
  San Jose, Costa Rica
Preedom, Richard Lawrence
  Columbia, South Carolina
Price, Robert Lee Jr.
  San Antonio, Texas
Prisby, James Christopher
  Hinsdale, Ilinois
Rauth, Ellen Marie
  Clarkston, Michigan
Rodriguez, Monica Thadine
  Stony Point, New York
Rossi, Geoffrey Allan
  Manchester, Massachusetts
Sablan, Vincent Edward
  Santa Rita, Guam

Schrader, Harry James
Huntington, New York

Smith, Theresa Marie
Westfield, New Jersey

Smyth, Evan Patrick
South Bend, Indiana

Tambor, Walter A.
Manalapan, New Jersey

Terrell, Jeffrey Dee
Streamwood, Illinois

Thomassen, James Lawrence
Newport Beach, California

Trerotola, Guy Anthony
Pine Brook, New Jersey

Vieira, Peter Francis Jr.
Villanova, Pennsylvania

Vizcarrondo Carrion,
Rosemarie
Guaynabo, Puerto Rico

Weldon, Kieran John
Fresno, California

Yung, Alan Sing Tak
Hong Kong

Master of Architecture

Hayes, Michael Thomas
South Bend, Indiana

Richmond, Kenneth Calvin
Sparta, Michigan

1991

Bachelor of Architecture

Andrea, John Sami
Baghdad, Iraq

Arends, Thomas David
Glens Falls, New York

Arroyo, Bernardo Oswaldo
Quito, Ecuador

Baraquio, Maria Lucy P.
Honolulu, Hawaii

Barnes, Maria Johanna
North Royalton, Ohio

Becker, Frank Xavier II
El Dorado, Kansas

Brink, Joseph Matthew
Pasadena, California

Chang, Wayne
Clifton Park, New York

Chiriboga, Rugel Fernando
Wharton, New Jersey

Conrard, Kimberly Marie
Cincinnati, Ohio

Dauplaise, Denise Marie
Green Bay, Wisconsin

Dearborn, Timothy Lee
Caribou, Maine

Delaune, Gregory Gerard
New Brighton, Minnesota

Dolan, Robert Steven
South Bend, Indiana

Donoghue, Timothy Howard
Manhattan, Kansas

Fletes, Luis Antonio
East Chicago, Indiana

Havel, Thomas Nicholas
Vallejo, California

Holdsworth, Gregg Alan
Williamsville, New York

Hubbard, Kevin Joseph
Elma, New York

Johnson, Steven Charles
San Antonio, Texas

Keim, Kevin Patrick
Natrona Heights,
Pennsylvania

Kim, Yong-Gap
South Bend, Indiana

Kirschner, Christopher Gary
Louisville, Kentucky

Lauer, Joseph Leo
Louisville, Kentucky

Lawson, Elaine Louise
South Bend, Indiana

Lyons, Daniel Edward
Albuquerque, New Mexico

Manfredy, John Ramon
East Chicago, Indiana

Mehl, Nicholas Jerome
Dallas, Texas

Mendoza, Angela Grace
El Paso, Texas

Miller, Michael William
Muskogee, Oklahoma

Moreno, Hector Eugenio
El Paso, Texas

Murphy, Scott Charles
Marlboro, Massachusetts

Perrella, Patrick Thomas
Princeton Junction,
New Jersey

Podrasky, Richard Wayne II
Silver Spring, Maryland

Polletta, Julie Christine
Aliquippa, Pennsylvania

Purcell, Mark Stephen
Upper Darby, Pennsylvania

Ramroth, Heidi
Dayton, Ohio

Salvon, Jonathan Michael
East Longmeadow,
Massachusetts

Thompson, Paula Louise
Grosse Pointe, Michigan

Tiller, Craig Lowell
Portage, Michigan

Treacy, James Vertume
Boxborough, Massachusetts

Master of Architecture

Doud, Eric L.
Davis, California

Foley, David Christian Carter
Pittsburgh, Pennsylvania

Pouler, Patrick J.
Trevor, Wisconsin

Singhal, Sanjay Raymond
Winthrop Harbor, Illinois

Wang, Yu
Beijing, China

1992

Bachelor of Architecture

Bagnoli, David Christopher
Ashland, Kentucky

Berjian, Stephanie Mary
Palm Beach Gardens, Florida

Bremhorst, Randy Mark
Philadelphia, Pennsylvania

Brennan, Michael Dillon
Kirkland, Illinois

Connolly, Michael Joseph
Warminster, Pennsylvania

Darin, John Joseph
Thousand Oaks, California

DeLave, Paul Sean
Grosse Pointe Farms,
Michigan

DiMario, Michael Paul
Lighthouse Point, Florida

Felton, Thomas Malcolm
Merion Station, Pennsylvania

Francoeur, Joan Elizabeth
Adrian, Michigan

Horne, Melody Lorita
Jackson, Mississippi

Ishak, Mohd Faid
Kelantan, Malaysia

Kelly, Sean Robert
Northboro, Massachusetts

Kletzly, Gregory Michael
Lakewood, Colorado

Kossler, James Kevin
Lithopolis, Ohio

Kruse, Christopher Dean
Peru, Nebraska

Kuhlman, David Christopher
Covington, Kentucky

Leik, Andrew Dennis
Portland, Michigan

Lopez, Maria Ines
Santiago, Chile

Maloney, Erin Chase
Pittsford, New York

Mateja, John David
West Hartford, Connecticut

Matiski, Vanessa J.
Superior, Wisconsin

Mayer, Bradley John
Minneapolis, Minnesota

McCaughey, Theresa L.
Chicago, Illinois

McGuire, James Corey
Ada, Oklahoma

McKinney, Kathleen Deanne
Allison Park, Pennsylvania

Montgomery, Jason Andrew
Pittsburgh, Pennsylvania

Nolte, Michael P.
Pensacola, Florida

Nowak, Stephen Thomas
South Bend, Indiana

Rakocy, Mary Elizabeth
Youngstown, Ohio

Shea, Carl W.
Ponte Vedra Beach, Florida

Slattery, Timothy Keenan
Rochester, New York

Squyres, Theresa Andrea
Glen Mills, Pennsylvania

Tinson, Albert James Jr.
Matthews, North Carolina

Valsaint, Fritz
Bridgeport, Connecticut

Weinkauf, Sarah Elizabeth
Houston, Texas

Wong, Jeanne
Poughkeepsie, New York

Wursthorn, Karla Rae
Mohnton, Pennsylvania

Zaloga, Jane Leslie
Notre Dame, Indiana

Zych, Kimberly Ann
Libertyville, Illinois

Master of Architecture

Deam, Christopher Charles
San Luis Obispo, California

Dong, Du
Beijing, China

Huderwitz, Francis Charles Jr.
Middletown, New Jersey

Kang, Lai-Yung
Taipei, Taiwan

Weber, Edward Eugene
Chicago, Illinois

1993

Bachelor of Architecture

Bartylla, Robert Charles
Phoenix, Arizona

Butler, Elizabeth Ann
Barrington, Illinois

DiChiara, Thomas Andrew
Redding, Connecticut

Ducar, John Robert
Batavia, Illinois

Etsitty, Deswood Clark
Pinon, Arizona

Fitzpatrick, Kelaine Marie
Columbus, Ohio

Genovese, Daniel Paul
Ridgewood, New Jersey

Green, Sean J.
Jacksonville, North Carolina

Halazon, Fawaz Raja
Amman, Jordan

Kasman, John Edward
Palos Heights, Illinois

Kinney, James Michael
Heath, Ohio

Klostermann, Douglas John
Chesterfield, Missouri

Lanahan, Thomas Joseph
Atlantis, Florida

Laucirica, Stephen Louis
Essex Fells, New Jersey

Lawson, Emily Jean
South Bend, Indiana

MacNeil, Katherine Marie
New Rochelle, New York

McGrath, Edward Charles
Panama City, Panama

McLaughlin, Kelly Marie
Birmingham, Alabama

Meyer, James Brendan
Scotch Plains, New Jersey

Miller, Michele L.
Wyomissing, Pennsylvania

Monberg, Gregory Hans
Hammond, Indiana

Murdy, Christopher John
Cherry Hills Village,
Colorado

Reyna, Marcelo Daniel
Springfield, New Jersey

Roman, Matthew Wayde
South Bend, Indiana

Sanderson, Mark Joseph
Wayne, Pennsylvania

Santulli, Mark Damon
Fayetteville, New York

Smith, Joseph Francis III
Vallejo, California

Sullivan, Shannon Elizabeth
Dayton, Ohio

Tepe, Manette A.
South Bend, Indiana

Thorell, Chandon Sherwood
Malvern, Pennsylvania

Vandevelde, John Anthony
La Canada, California

Viola, Joseph Yoshimitsu
Rancho Palos Verde,
California

Westervelt, Joel Drake
Camp Verde, Arizona

Wong, Andrea Kim
South Bend, Indiana

Yoshizu, Sherri Kiku
Cypress, California

Master of Architecture

Aquino Lichauco, Daniel V.
Quezon City, Philippines

Franck, Michael M.
Florence, Alabama

Klund, Jennifer
Anoka, Minnesota

Torres-Cruz, Jaime
Santa Fe de Bogota,
Colombia

1994

Bachelor of Architecture

Adrian, Marcus Edward
St. Louis, Missouri

Bellalta, Diego Jose
South Bend, Indiana

Casas, Braulio Leo
Chula Vista, California

Chandler, Azikiwe Terry
Charleston, South Carolina

Cluver, John Henry
Broomall, Pennsylvania

Colgan, David Thomas
William
Augusta, Georgia

Collins, Brian Paul
Mendon, Massachusetts

DelVecchio, Melissa Lynn
Stratford, Connecticut

Dingle, Mary Jean
Catonsville, Maryland

Egan, Nicole Michele
Niles, Illinois

Galles, Heidi Marie
Cedar Rapids, Iowa

Graves, Carolyn Granger
Coos Bay, Oregon

Heit, David Scott
Topeka, Kansas

Hernandez, Andrea A.
Buenos Aires, Argentina

Howard, Andrew D.
Bronx, New York

Jones, Kevin Louis
Holland, Michigan

Koenig, Gregory Otto
Ketchum, Idaho

Lee, Dean Bruce
Lagrange, Indiana

Liporto, Michael Paul
North Andover,
Massachusetts

Mazurek, Jeffrey M.
Cheektowaga, New York

McDougall, Jennifer Louise
Kent, Washington

Mitchell, Brian Dennis
West Des Moines, Iowa

Mizelle, Holly Lynn
Columbus, Ohio

Moore, David Lawrence
Anchorage, Alaska

Norian, Elizabeth Katherine
Middlebury, Vermont

Perez, Alejo
Port Hueneme, California

Quigley, Carol Jean
West Chester, Pennsylvania

Rich, Brian DeMars
Seattle, Washington

Rogers, Clarke M.
Orinda, California

Smith, Kimberlee Lynn
Mount Prospect, Illinois

Sorrentino, Matthew
Northport, New York

Steindorf, Stephanie Ann
Madison, Wisconsin

van Koolbergen, Martin James
Montvale, New Jersey

Master of Architecture

Bolgar, Benjamin J.
Essex, England

Franck, Christine Gardner
Huckins
Washington, D.C.

1995

Bachelor of Architecture

Beaton, Michael J.
Utica, New York

Blough, Jeffrey Michael
Pittsburgh, Pennsylvania

Caddigan, Robert Alan
Randolph, Massachusetts

Casas Zurita, Ricardo
El Paso, Texas

Chiu, Clement Yu Hin
Hong Kong

Denver, Molly Kathryn
Tequesta, Florida

DiGiacomo, Marc
Dallas, Texas

Dingle, Harry Jules
Baltimore, Maryland

Dudick, John Allan Jr.
Grand Rapids, Michigan

Dumais, Christopher A.
Lewiston, Maine

Gedney, Joshua Scott
Louisville, Kentucky

Gordon, Eileen Marie
Annapolis, Maryland

Hankins, Karen E.
Germantown, Tennessee

Howard, Thomas John Jr.
Houston, Texas

Lardinois, Sara Ann
Green Bay, Wisconsin

Lau, Hok-Sze
Hong Kong

Lauinger, Elizabeth Jeanne
Tulsa, Oklahoma

Mellor, John Christopher
Omaha, Nebraska

Musty, Peter J.
Brainerd, Minnesota

Nathe, David Montgomery
Waynesboro, Virginia

Parolek, Daniel Gerard
Columbus, Nebraska

Price, Eliot Walter
Waverly, Ohio

Roberts, Joseph Lanier
South Bend, Indiana

Rottinghaus, Gayle Frances
Seneca, Kansas

Saavedra, Victor M.
Mishawaka, Indiana

Schaupp, Richard Harry
Kinnelon, New Jersey

Shinnefield, Meaghan
Maureen
La Habra, California

Siwek, Peter Christopher
Augusta, Kansas

Thompson, Cheryl Lee
Elmira, New York

Wingerter, Lori Jean
Erie, Pennsylvania

Wong, Santiago Alejo
Port Jefferson, New York

Yang, Frank Fu-Jen
South Bend, Indiana

Yinh, Juan A.
Panama City, Panama

Zureikat, Lara
Amman, Jordan

Master of Architecture

Chrisman, Stephen T.
Salem, Oregon

Savic, Nebojsa
Belgrade, Yugoslavia

Waldman, Noah Andrew
Rydal, Pennsylvania

1996

Bachelor of Architecture

Alvarez-Diaz, Ricardo A.
San Juan, Puerto Rico

Beck, Charles Daniel
Freehold, New Jersey

Boita, Cristina Elizabeth
Rochester, New York

Bridgewater, Susan Lynn
Brownsville, Texas

Brooks, Nick
Bloomfield, Connecticut

Bucci, Andrew John
Elmira, New York

Capo, Michael
Wayne, New Jersey

Cook, Daniel Wade
Oklahoma City, Oklahoma

Cruz, Johnny Jr.
Seguin, Texas

Cully, Manda Jean
Coldwater, Ohio

Davidson, Ross Alan
Belleville, Illinois

Diez, Marco A.
Santo Domingo,
Dominican Republic

Estrada Ramirez, Tomas
Dededo, Guam

Fitzgerald, Matthew Joachim
Pittsburgh, Pennsylvania

Gago, Marianela
Panama City, Panama

Gallagher, Jennifer Lynn
Youngstown, Ohio

Goussous, Rana Haitham
South Bend, Indiana

Greenberg, Peter
Guilford, Connecticut

Guze, Brian Charles
Eden Prarie, Minnesota

Hartz, Christopher Roger
  Menomonie, Wisconsin
Irby, Ericka Da'Shun
  South Holland, Illinois
Kanaras, Nicholas
  Granby, Connecticut
Kaywood, Thomas
  Lawrence Jr.
  Grand Rapids, Michigan
Kleczewski, Duane Thomas
  Sleepy Hollow, Illinois
Malpass, Kevin Patrick
  Erie, Pennsylvania
McDonnell, Eileen Margaret
  Quincy, Massachusetts
Mesko, Michael Stephen
  Potomac, Maryland
Milligan, Colleen Elizabeth
  Summerville, South Carolina
Musielewicz, John Theodore
  Britton, Michigan
Nageswaran, Ruchira Dileep
  Colorado Springs, Colorado
Pellegrini, Stefan Dante
  Muncie, Indiana
Rios Reyes, Ilia Maria
  Rio Piedras, Puerto Rico
Schmitt, Lisa Lynn
  Cambridge, Wisconsin
Sockalosky, Evan Thomas
  St. Paul, Minnesota
Steinhauer, David Blaine
  Mishawaka, Indiana
Sullivan, Daniel Patrick
  Winterset, Iowa
Summers, Aaron Vincent
  Wright Patterson AFB, Ohio
Tran, Uyen To
  Kirkland, Washington
Walbridge, Lisa Marie
  Scituate, Massachusetts
Whitfield, LaTonya Trichelle
  Prairie View, Texas

Master of Architecture

Casas, Braulio
  San Diego, California
Hook, Timothy Justin
  Hertfordshire, England
McRoberts, Duncan
  McCallum
  Portland, Oregon
Petkovic, Milan S.
  Belgrade, Yugoslavia
Pilla, Robert John
  Stuart, Florida
Strus, Allan
  Tallinn, Estonia

1997

Bachelor of Architecture

Arnold, Douglas Jason
  Pittsburgh, Pennsylvania

Bailly, Marc Ernest
  Windsor, California
Brockhagen, Alexander
  Christian
  Phoenix, Arizona
Carnahan, Chad Michael
  Raeford, North Carolina
Christensen, Erik Ronald
  Indianapolis, Indiana
Creech, Diana Lefever
  Columbia City, Indiana
Curran, Kevin Matthew
  Jefferson, South Dakota
Cusato, Marianne
  Anchorage, Alaska
Czajkowski, Andrew Paul
  Ponte Vedra Beach, Florida
DuBose, Broderick Benjel
  Gary, Indiana
Eatinger, Charlene Diane
  El Centro, California
Fashek, Christiane Michael
  San Antonio, Texas
Gage, Mark Foster
  Omaha, Nebraska
Gallo, Cristiana
  Dayton, Ohio
Garza, Petra Analia
  Cotulla, Texas
Gonzalez Acevedo, Maria
  del Carmen
  Guayaquil, Ecuador
Goodall, Todd Henry
  San Diego, California
Jager, Jerusha Erin
  San Jose, California
Kane, Brian Thomas
  Pensacola, Florida
Kim, Malaika Nicole
  South Bend, Indiana
McCarthy, Bernadette C.
  Brockton, Massachusetts
McConaghy, Dawn Kristen
  West Warwick, Rhode Island
Molaison, Danielle Rose
  Houma, Louisiana
Moran, Erin Day
  Louisville, Kentucky
Mufti, Lemis
  Amman, Jordan
Mulcahy, Robert Gerard
  Rumson, New Jersey
Nohelty, Sean Patrick
  Des Plaines, Illinois
Papadopoulos, Stella Ann
  Des Plaines, Illinois
Peschel, Andrea Emilia
  Minneapolis, Minnesota
Pledger, Mark Edward
  Birmingham, Alabama
Ponce, Maria Teresa
  Quito, Ecuador
Quiroga Corvalan, Nahuel
  Santiago, Chile

Rengel, Mark Thomas
  Superior, Wisconsin
Sacksteder, Mary Rebecca
  Dayton, Ohio
Seiling, Derek Bartel
  Pittsburgh, Pennsylvania
Shveima, Michael Francis
  Bartlesville, Oklahoma
Slaunwhite, Deborah
  Elizabeth
  Orchard Park, New York
Sobalvarro Rosales,
  Armando A.
  Guatemala City, Guatemala
Sromek, Amy Marie
  Anderson, Indiana
Tantash, Lina Farouk
  Amman, Jordan
Terry, Amina Nadeen
  St. Louis, Missouri
Tremblay, Jocelyn
  Beaufort, South Carolina
Vu, Hoa Thai
  Omaha, Nebraska
Wendel, Mark James
  Lancaster, New York

Master of Architecture

Finn, Christine E.
  Marblehead, Massachusetts
He, Keren
  Beijing, China
Murrill, Stephanie Ann
  Wilmington, North Carolina
Robbins, Ashley Lawren
  Galax, Virginia
She, Rongchang
  Fujian, China

1998

Bachelor of Architecture

Apostolou, Alexandra
  Elizabeth
  Pittsburgh, Pennsylvania
Arosemena, Ricardo
  Panama City, Panama
Bossardt, Laura Anne
  Wayzata, Minnesota
Brown, Christopher R.
  Cranston, Rhode Island
Connor, Margaret Mary
  Columbus, Ohio
Cruz, Joseph Henry
  Olney, Maryland
Failla, MaryBeth
  Pittsburgh, Pennsylvania
Garlock, Matthew Philip
  Lima, Ohio
Gomez, Carlos
  El Paso, Texas
Gulling, Dana Kathleen
  Green Bay, Wisconsin
Hoenle, Shelley Lynn
  Woodbridge, Virginia

Hoffman, Adrianne Marie
  Fort Wayne, Indiana
Locksmith, Geoffrey P.
  Augusta, Georgia
Loftus, Brian Patrick
  Margate, New Jersey
McManus, Thomas Joseph III
  Westford, Massachusetts
Melone, Nicholas R.
  Wilkes-Barre, Pennsylvania
Molina, Stefan J.
  Odessa, Texas
Muzikir, Abdul
  Silver Spring, Maryland
Noethe, Jan Eva
  Middlebury, Indiana
Orrantia, Maria Cecilia
  Guayaquil, Ecuador
Podstawski, Christopher John
  South Amboy, New Jersey
Propes, Aimee
  Portales, New Mexico
Reynaert, Jennifer Leigh
  Rochester, Michigan
Rice, Jennifer Lynn
  Herndon, Virginia
Rodriguez, David Manuel
  Panama City, Panama
Samora, Manuel Damian
  Colorado Springs, Colorado
Shea, Laura M.
  Fargo, North Dakota
Sobol, Jennifer Anne
  Richmond, Indiana
Soundy, Marie Andree
  Guatemala City, Guatemala
Stanton, Robert Anthony
  Detroit, Michigan
Ting, Shirley Vai
  Scarborough, Ontario
Torres, Alejandra
  Hidalgo, Texas
Warnke, Charlton Joseph
  Elk City, Oklahoma
Welsh, Jeremy Matthew
  Moon Township,
  Pennsylvania

Master of Architecture

Deegan, Edward James
  Flossmoor, Illinois
Devemy, Cecile Marie
  La Ferte-Milon, France
Heydt, Charles Otto III
  Atlanta, Georgia
Huang, Yin
  Chongqing, China
Marano, Thomas Michael
  Dillonvale, Ohio
Mesko, Michael Stephen
  Potomac, Maryland
Punnoose, George K.
  Kerala, India
Tobin, Sean Jefferson
  Osterville, Massachusetts

Figure 101.

The Undergraduate Class of 1999.

Blanchet-Ruth, Carlo
  South Bend, Indiana
Cutler, David
  Seattle, Washington
Dwyer, Michael
  Elmhurst, Illinois
Ebert, Edward
  Incline Village, Nevada
Epstein, Grant
  Chicago, Illinois
Ertel, Mallory
  St. Charles, Illinois
Gaskin, Danjuma
  Chicago, Illinois
Goldsby, Anthony
  Springfield, Illinois
Kawashima, Ayako
  Tokyo, Japan
McCormac, Philip
  Phoenix, Arizona
Meier, Christopher
  Fort Wayne, Indiana
Morgan, Jeffrey
  Spiceland, Indiana
Printup, Bryan
  Sanborn, New York

Riley, Colleen
  Florham Park, New Jersey
Schuth, Kathryn
  Bloomington, Indiana
Sullivan, Michael
  Orland Park, Illinois
Uresti, Jesus
  Ecorse, Michigan
Vignali, Christy
  Ottawa, Illinois

Not pictured:

Butchko, Kristy
  O'Fallon, Illinois
Delaney, Sheila
  Indiana, Pennslyvania
Janson, Christopher
  Green Lane, Pennslyvania
Perez-Franceschini, Isabel
  Guaynabo, Puerto Rico
Soundy, Roberto
  Guatemala, Guatemala
Wiberg, Kathleen
  North Oaks, Minnesota

Figure 102.

The Graduate Class of 1999.

Carapella, Carmine
  Rome, Italy
Dodd, Philip
  Bury, England
Feng, Weiqing
  Beijing, China
Onyango, John
  Nairobi, Kenya
Wang, Hai
  Tianjing, China

Table of Illustrations

Figure 1. Laurens Paul Cotter. An Aquarium. 1929
(Notre Dame Archives) .... facing page 1

Figure 2. Manufactures and Liberal Arts Building, 1893
World's Columbian Exposition, Chicago
(Notre Dame Archives) 5

Figure 3. Architecture drafting studio on the
Administration Building's fifth floor, 1914
(Notre Dame Archives) 7

Figure 4. Henry John Schlacks (Archdiocese of Chicago.
The New World, 14 April 1900, 4) 7

Figure 5. Francis Xavier Ackerman (*The Dome,* 1906) 7

Figure 6. The art department studio on the
Administration Building's fifth floor, 1905
(Notre Dame Archives) 8

Figure 7. Eugenio P. Rayneri y Piedra (Notre Dame
Archives) 9

Figure 8. Eugenio P. Rayneri y Piedra. First-floor plan
of an unnamed building, 1904
(Notre Dame Archives) 9

Figure 9. Edward Rolland Adelsperger
(*The Dome,* 1906) 10

Figure 10. Francis Wynn Kervick, c1909
(Notre Dame Archives) 11

Figure 11. Paul Anthony Rigali. A Greek Doric
Hexastyle-Peripteral Temple, 1933
(Notre Dame Archives) 12

Figure 12. The Architects' Club on the Administration
Building steps, 1911 (*The Dome,* 1911) 13

Figure 13. The Architects' Club, 1918
(*The Dome,* 1918) 14

Figure 14. Frank Montana
(*The Dome,* 1940) 15

Figure 15. Ambrose Richardson
(Notre Dame Archives) 16

Figure 16. Robert L. Amico
(Notre Dame Photographic Services) 16

Figure 17. Robert J. Schultz. Piazza Navona, Roma,
c1970 (Courtesy of Geri Decker) 17

Figure 18. Karl A. Krueger. Sant'Ivo della Sapienza,
Rome, 1987 (Courtesy of Donald Sporleder) 18

Figure 19. Frank Montana. Roman Forum, 27 October
1980 (Courtesy of Frank Montana) 18

Figure 20. Dana Gulling. Geneva Terrace, Chicago.
Plan, elevation and section, 1997 19

Figure 21. Manuel Damian Samora. West Kemper Street
elevation, Chicago, 1997 19

Figure 22. Andrea Emilia Peschel. Slovak Cultural
and Spiritual Center, Minneapolis, Minnesota,
1997 20

Figure 23. A drawing class, 1953
(*The Dome,* 1953) .... facing page 25

Figure 24. The Administration Building, c1900
(Notre Dame Archives) 26

Figure 25. The Architecture Building
(now Crowley Hall of Music), c1920
(Notre Dame Archives) 27

Figure 26. Inauguration of the renovated
Lemonnier Library building, 1 May 1965
(Notre Dame Archives) 28

Figure 27. Foyer of the Architecture Building, c1969
(Notre Dame Archives) 28

Figure 28. Bond Hall inauguration, 21 March 1997
(Notre Dame Photographic Services) 29

Figure 29. Honorary degree recipients Porphyrios,
Plater-Zyberk and Greenberg
(Notre Dame Photographic Services) 29

Figure 30. The Lemonnier Library card catalog room,
c1960 (Notre Dame Archives) 30

Figure 31. Bond Hall before the renovation
(Photo: Dennis P. Doordan) 31

Figures 32 and 33. Bond Hall, fall 1997
(Photo: Jon Miller, Hedrich Blessing Photographers;
Architecture Library Collection) 32

Figure 34. In the fourth-year studio, Bond Hall, 1999
(Photo: Matt Cashore) 33

Figure 35. Rome Studies Center inaugural celebration,
16 January 1986 (Courtesy of Bob Amico) 34

Figure 36. The Rome Studies Center, Via Monterone,
1999 (Photo: Tony Kelly) 34

Figure 37. The Architects' Club on the
Administration Building steps, 1920
(*The Dome,* 1920) .... facing page 37

Figure 38. The Architects' Club outside the Rockne
Memorial, 1949 (*The Dome,* 1949) .... facing page 37

Figure 39. George A. Beltemacchi. An Etruscan Gate,
1936 (Notre Dame Archives) 38

Figure 40. Francis Kervick (*The Dome,* 1930) 39

Figure 41. Kervick & Fagan Architects, Lyons Hall,
east elevation, 1925 (Notre Dame Archives) 39

Figure 42. William Laffan. Building for a Glass
Distributor, 1951 (Notre Dame Archives) 40

Figure 43. Frank Montana during his Paris Prize year,
1936 (Courtesy of Frank Montana) 42

Figure 44. Frank Montana. Guérande, France,
14 August 1937 (Courtesy of Frank Montana) 43

Figure 45. Vito Girone (*The Dome,* 1953) 44

Figure 46. Aladar Olgyay (*The Dome,* 1948) 44

Figure 47. Victor Olgyay (*The Dome,* 1948) 44

Figure 48. Otto Seeler (*The Dome,* 1953) 44

Figure 49. Ernst Brandl (*The Dome,* 1953) 44

Figure 50. Paul Grillo leads a class discussion in
studio, c1956 (Notre Dame Archives) 45

Figure 51. Ventura Gonzalez. A House in Texas,
c1947 (Notre Dame Archives) 46

Figure 52. Richard Scott Kirk. A Nursery Unit of a
School, 1949 (Notre Dame Archives) 46

Figure 53. C. Arnold Thoma, Class of 1928
(*The Dome,* 1928) 49

Figure 54. Class of 2000 students in the Bond Hall
fourth-year studio
(Photo: Matt Cashore) .... facing page 51

Figure 55. Robert L. Amico (Photo: Matt Cashore) 53

Figure 56. The Kinetic Skyscraper® team, 1999
(Photo: Matt Cashore) 54

Figures 57 and 58. Research, and Special Project in
Advanced Design, 1986 55

Figures 59, 60 and 61. Design Thesis, 1995; and
Design Thesis Development, 1996 56

Figures 62 and 63. Research, and Special Project in
Advanced Design, 1998– 57

Figures 64 and 65. Design Thesis, 1992. 58

Figures 66 and 67. Special Project in Advanced
Design, 1997 58

Figure 68. Marie Andree Soundy. Sant'Agnese,
Piazza Navona, Roma, 1995 .... facing page 61

Figure 69. Thomas Gordon Smith on the steps of
the Architecture Building, 1995
(Photo: Matt Cashore) 63

Figure 70. James Canizaro. Title page for
*The Architectural Work of Graham, Anderson,
Probst & White, Chicago,* 1933
(Architecture Library Collection) .... facing page 65

Figure 71. The Architects' Club in the
Administration Building fifth-floor studio, 1912
(*The Dome,* 1912) 66

Figure 72. Ida Bonicelli in the Architecture Library,
c1947 (Courtesy of Mary Yolanda Trigiani) 68

Figure 73. The Architecture Library in its third
location, c1970 (Courtesy of Geri Decker) 69

Figure 74. Librarian Geri Decker in her office, c1970
(Courtesy of Geri Decker) 70

Figures 75 and 76. Bookplates for the Shaheen and
Wamser Endowments. 71

Figure 77. The Rare Book Room, 1997
(Photo: Richard Pare; School of
Architecture Collection) 72

Figure 78. The new Architecture Library, 1997
(Photo: Jon Miller, Hedrich Blessing Photographers;
Architecture Library Collection) 73

Figure 79. Vito Girone corrects a student's drawing,
1949 (*The Dome,* 1949) .... facing page 76

Figure 80. Julian Kulski and students review plans for a
proposed redevelopment of downtown Michigan
City, 1962 (Notre Dame Archives) 79

Figure 81. Frank Montana, Kenneth Featherstone,
Donald Sporleder and Brian Crumlish, c1968
(Notre Dame Archives) 79

Figure 82. Samir Younés and Norman Crowe
with students, 1998 (Photo: Notre Dame
Undergraduate Admissions) 79

Figure 83. Outside the Forum, Rome, 1984 92

Figure 84. Ostia Antica, 1996
(Photo: Kathryn Schuth) 92

Figure 85. At Hadrian's Villa, 1996
(Photo: Kathryn Schuth) 92

Figure 86. Albergo Lunetta, 1997
(Photo: Kathryn Schuth) 92

Figure 87. Temple of Hera, Sicily, 1978
(Photo: Norman A. Crowe) 92

Figure 88. Beaux-Arts Ball, 1956 (*The Dome,* 1956) 93

Figure 89. Beaux-Arts Ball, 1958 (*The Dome,* 1958) 93

Figure 90. Beaux-Arts Ball, 1957 (*The Dome,* 1957) 93

Figure 91. Beaux-Arts Ball in Rome, 1973 (Photo:
Williston Dye) 93

Figure 92. Beaux-Arts Ball, 1958 (*The Dome,* 1958) 93

Figure 93. Beaux-Arts Ball in Rome, 1996
(Photo: Kathryn Schuth) 93

Figure 94. Wielding t-squares in the studio, 1950
(*The Dome,* 1950) 94

Figure 95. At the drafting table, 1957
(Notre Dame Archives) 94

Figure 96. On the construction site, Chicago, 1980
(Photo: Norman A. Crowe) 94

Figure 97. Reynolds Aluminum Prize winners, 1961
(Notre Dame Archives) 94

Figure 98. The Graduate Class of 1997
(Photo: Norman A. Crowe) 95

Figure 99. In the fourth-year studio, 1999
(Photo: Matt Cashore) 95

Figure 100. Commencement Day, 1998
(Photo: Andrew Campbell) 95

Figure 101. The Undergraduate Class of 1999
(Photo: Matt Cashore) 103

Figure 102. The Graduate Class of 1999
(Photo: Matt Cashore) 103

Index

Page numbers in *italics* indicate illustrations.

A

Ackerman, Francis Xavier 7
Adelsperger, Edward Rolland *10, 13*
Administration Building 6, *7, 8, 26*, 27, *66*
Amico Architecture Scholarship 59
Amico, Robert *16, 34, 53*
Anderson, Peirce 13
Architects' Club *13, 14, facing page 37, 66*
Architecture Building *See*
    Bond Hall
    Crowley Hall
    Lemonnier Library
Art Deco 15
Art Department *8, 9*

B

Babcock, Charles 4
Baldo, Luis 55
Basilica of the Sacred Heart 13
Beaux-Arts Institute of Design 13, 14, 15, 40, 41,
    42, 45, 46
Bellalta, Esmée 16
Belluschi, Pietro *28*
Beltemacchi, George 37, *38*
Bond, William and Joanne *29*, 53, 63
Bond Hall *See also* Lemonnier Library 29, *32, 33, 63*
Bond-Montedonico Fellowship 53
Bonicelli, Ida *68*, 69
Bonicelli, Irma 68
Brandl, Ernst 44, 45
Brandt, Robert 33
Burgee, John and Gwen 72
Burgee, Joseph Z. Fellowship 53
Burnham, Daniel 5, 6
Byrne, Paul 67

C

C.F. Murphy & Associates 16
Café Poché 33
Canizaro, James *facing page 65*, 71
Center for Continuing Education 15
Chicago Architecture Center 53
City Beautiful Movement 6, 13
Classicism 20, 21
College of Commerce 13
College of Engineering 13, 16, 19, 59, 71
Columbia University 4, 5, 10, 53
Columbkille, Brother, C.S.C. 27
Cornell University 4
Cotter, Laurens Paul *facing page 1*

Cram, Ralph Adams 39
Cram & Ferguson 13
Crowe, Norman 16, *79*
Crowley Hall *6, 27*, 28, 67
Crumlish, Brian *79*
Cushing Hall of Engineering 13

D

Decker, Geri *70*
Diez, Marco *56*
Durand, J.-N.-L. *8, 9*

E

École des Beaux-Arts 3, 15, 29, 42
Ecumenical Institute (Jerusalem) 15
Edbrooke, Willoughby J. 6, 27
Ellerbe-Becket Associates 29
Fagan, Vincent 13, *14*, 39
Fashek, Christiane *58*
Featherstone, Kenneth *79*
Fischer Von Erlach, J.B. 9
Furniture design program 33

G

Gay, Norman *28*
Girone, Vito 44, *76*
Goldsby, Anthony 59
Gonzalez, Ventura *46*
Graham, Anderson, Probst & White 11, 13
Graham, Ernest 11, 71
Greenberg, Allan *29*
Grillo, Paul *45*
Gulling, Dana *19*

H

Hansen, Harold M. 4
Harvard University 4
Havlik, Robert 71
Hesburgh, Rev. Theodore M., C.S.C. *28, 34, 51*
Hoenle, Shelley *57*
Horsbrugh, Patrick 16, 70
Howard Hall 13
Hoynes Hall *See* Crowley Hall
Hunt, Richard Morris 3
Hurtt, Steven 16

I

Indianapolis Museum of Art 16
Institute of Technology 6, 27

K

Kawneer Prize   40
Keating, Daniel   *55*
Kervick, Francis Wynn   *11, 13, 14,* 30, *39,* 67, 68
Kim, Malika   *58*
Kirk, Richard Scott   *46*
Krannert Museum of Art   16
Krueger, Karl   18
Kulski, Julian   69, *79*

L

Laffan, William   38
Lavanoux, Maurice   46
Lemonnier Library   *See also* Bond Hall   28, *30,* 31
Létang, Eugène   *4*
Locksmith, Geoffrey   *57*
Lyons Hall   13, *39*

M

Main Building   *See* Administration Building
Malloy, Rev. Edward, C.S.C.   *29,* 54
Manfredi, Michael A.   16
Marr, Alfredo   *55*
Martelli, Rev. Jose, C.S.C.   34
Massachusetts Institute of Technology   4, 10
McKim, Mead & White   29, 30
Michel, Anthony   63
Miller, John E.   14
Milonadis, Tobi   69
Modernism   15, 21, 38, 41
Montana, Frank   *15, 18,* 28, *34, 42,* 43, 53, 68, *79*
Morrissey Hall   13

N

Noethe, Jan   *58*

O

O'Shaughnessy, Mary   72
O'Toole, Mary   *55*
Olgyay, Aladar   44
Olgyay, Victor   44

P

Paradis, Jobson Emilien   *9*
Paris Prize   15, 16, 42
Peschel, Andrea Emilia   *20*
Plater-Zyberk, Elizabeth   *29*
Plym Endowment   71
Porphyrios, Demetri   *29*
Propes, Aimee   *58*

R

Rabb, Maxwell   34
Rayneri y Piedra, Eugenio P.   *9*
Rice, Jennifer   *57*
Richardson, Ambrose   *16,* 52
Rigali, Paul Anthony   *12*
Rogers, John Gamble   13
Rome Studies Center   15, 16, 17, 18, *34,* 43, 53, 62
Rowe, Colin   16
Ryan Family   72

S

Samora, Manuel Damian   *19*
Schlacks, Henry John   *7*
Schmitz, Roger   16
Schultz, Robert J.   15, *17*
Seeler, Otto   44, 53
Shaheen, Eli J. and Helen Endowment   71
Skidmore, Owings & Merrill   16
Slattery, Timothy   *58*
Smith, Thomas Gordon   19, 20, 21, *29,* 33, *63,* 72
Snite Museum of Art   16
Society of Beaux-Arts Architects   40
Soundy, Marie Andree   *facing page 61*
South Bend (Indiana)   6
South Dining Hall   13, *39*
Sporleder, Donald   *79*
Sprague, Paul   69

T

Tigerman, Stanley   61
Tilton, Edward   11, 29, 30

U

University Club   15
University of Illinois at Urbana-Champaign   4, 16, 51

V

Van Brunt, Henry   3, 5

W

Wamser, Thomas and Anne Family Endowment   71
Ware, William Robert   4, 10, 11
Warren, Herbert Langford   4, 8
Warren, Lloyd   14
Wesoloski, Alice   final page
Wright, Frank Lloyd   71
World's Columbian Exposition   *5,* 6

Y

Younés, Samir   *79*

Z

Zahm, Rev. John, C.S.C.   6

IN APPRECIATION

The story of the School of Architecture
would not be complete without a
special tribute to

Alice Wesoloski.

Alice has been secretary to four
chairmen, administrator, counselor,
problem-solver extraordinaire and
true friend to the students and faculty
from 1958 until her retirement in 1998.